ESSAYS ON MALORY

ESSAYS ON MALORY

BY

WALTER OAKESHOTT, C. S. LEWIS
EUGENE VINAVER, D. S. BREWER
P. E. TUCKER, F. WHITEHEAD
SALLY SHAW

Edited by

J. A. W. BENNETT

CLARENDON PRESS · OXFORD
1963

Oxford University Press, Amen House, London E.C.4
GLASGOW NEW YORK TORONTO MELBOURNE WELLINGTON
BOMBAY CALCUTTA MADRAS KARACHI LAHORE DACCA
CAPE TOWN SALISBURY NAIROBI IBADAN ACCRA
KUALA LUMPUR HONG KONG

Printed in Great Britain by
The Camelot Press Ltd., London and Southampton

Preface

THE publication in 1947 of Professor Vinaver's edition of Malory, an edition based on the unique and long-lost manuscript and enriched with an extensive and magistral commentary, gave a fresh impetus to Arthurian and in particular to Malorian studies. The consequent undulations have not yet died away, and their marks are plain to see in Professor Loomis's many-sided symposium on *Arthurian Literature in the Middle Ages* (1959). Yet in that European survey Malory and his book could be granted only a dozen pages. To say that those pages are from Professor Vinaver's pen is to say that they are the best introduction to 'the hoole book of Kyng Arthur' now in print. But his reference to studies set in motion by his edition had to be confined to a footnote; and though a few of the studies in the present volume had been adumbrated none was completed or accessible when that footnote was written.

This volume may therefore be regarded as a product of twelve years' attention to Professor Vinaver's edition, as an extension of his chapter on *A.L.M.A.*, and as a tribute to his criticism and his scholarship. Not least of his merits as a critic is his readiness to take account of points of view differing from his own; and this could hardly be better shown than in the debate with Professor Lewis here for the first time set forth. Several of the points raised in that debate are pursued or reconsidered in the succeeding essays. Though several of these studies were initiated at Oxford, the contributors represent no single school of thought. The volume is not a collaborative effort, and no attempt has been made to tone down differences; but these may turn out to be differences of emphasis rather than of outlook; and while all the essayists may not sing to the same tune, there is perhaps a *discordia concors*.

It will certainly be apparent that despite the renewal of Malorian studies in this country and—witness the Bibliographical Note—in the United States, 'a large field is yet left unto sharper discerners'. Some parts of that field have already been marked out, but others have barely been surveyed. Thus we are hardly equipped as yet to make a thorough analysis of Malory's style, or styles. It is easy enough to show that in his fifth book he was under the spell of the alliterative *Morte* and that in his last there are phrases and rhythms that come straight from the stanzaic *Morte*. But no one has yet attempted a detailed comparison of his prose with that of the French texts that were the bases of the greater part of his book—nor with that of the English *Merlin*, the only vernacular prose romance known to us that could have been known to Malory, but one that reproduces French sentence-patterns and word-order far more closely than he usually does. And to trace his successors—except in latter-day pastiche—is as difficult as to find his forerunners. Lord Berners, to be sure, comes at once to mind; but in Berners two elements that in Malory are confused—or fused—have become distinct: Berners the romancer writes *Huon of Bordeaux* and *Arthur of Little Britain*, far outdoing Malory in *faerie*; Berners the knight translates Froissart magnificently, being perhaps more at ease with French and French chivalry than Malory ever was. Yet a study of the differences (however minor) in the chivalry of the two knightly authors might make it easier to distinguish the specifically English qualities in Malory's code, which in its ethics, its political and social ideals, its very utterances, sometimes reveals affinities with the world of Layamon and even the world of *Beowulf* and *Maldon*.

The plan of the present volume does not allow us to consider what part scholarship has played in extending the appeal of the Arthurian story within the last two decades. But the most austere scholar must rejoice that thanks to talents as various as those of Eugene Vinaver, Charles Williams, and T. H. White, Malory is today read more widely than ever before, and perhaps with greater sympathy than at any time since Spenser. When the discovery of the manuscript was announced in the curious circumstances described by the Rector of Lincoln in the following pages, Professor Vinaver was followed to Winchester (if report is true) by an aircraftman on a motor-cycle: the author of *The Seven Pillars of Wisdom* had it in mind to make his own version of the *Morte*. Report likewise says that a writer of such different cast as Mr. John Steinbeck will one day offer us his highly individual recension of the Vinaver text. Professor Lewis's image of the Arthurian cathedral with elements that 'grow together into something strange and admirable which none of its successive builders intended or foresaw' thus seems likely to retain its aptness.

J. A. W. B.

St. Swithun's Day, 1961.

Contents

I

The Finding of the Manuscript

W. F. OAKESHOTT

THE identification of the Winchester manuscript of the *Morte Darthur* in 1934 was the result of a fortunate series of accidents. The College Library at that time consisted, as to some extent it still does, of two different entities, the Fellows' Library, having a continuous history going back to the foundation of the College, and Moberly Library, established in the nineteenth century for the use of ordinary members of the school. It does not seem to have occurred to Fellows, or to headmasters, in the seventeenth and eighteenth centuries, that any library should be accessible to boys, or even to assistant masters, and not till the mid-nineteenth century was Moberly Library established to fill this need. Both libraries have had their vicissitudes during the last hundred years. 'It is appalling', one of the Fellows once remarked in my hearing, 'how the books get rushed around from place to place. There have been no less than four moves of this library during the last five centuries.' In 1934 the Fellows' Library was housed, as it still is, in the gallery of the Warden's Lodgings. I became Librarian of Moberly Library at the time when the reconstruction of the medieval Brewery by Sir Herbert Baker as the new Moberly Library was being planned, the originator of the plan being the then Headmaster, Dr. A. T. P. Williams.

One feature which we planned for the new library from the first was the provision in it of a number of showcases. For already from my undergraduate days I had been interested in early printed books and in manuscripts. Access to the Fellows' Library even in 1934 was not easy for the ordinary assistant master. But I had won the confidence of the Librarian, who let me have the run of the open shelves for a study of the sixteenth-century bindings which I was then making. This was instigated by J. B. Oldham, Librarian of Shrewsbury School, now well known as a leading authority in this field. He already knew more than most people about blind stamped fifteenth and sixteenth century bindings though his work was then only in its early stages. Spurred on by him, I had made rubbings of many of the Oxford or Cambridge or London bindings of the early sixteenth century that were readily accessible, and I already knew which of them when pulled out of the shelves showered one with a fine brown powder from boards that were riddled with worm, and was already planning a campaign of preservation. In the course of looking for bindings, however, I had become increasingly impressed with the possibilities of the Fellows' Library for teaching purposes. There was, for example, a remarkable series of travel books and atlases even on the open shelves. It was often my job to teach sixteenth-century history. How satisfactory it would be to be able to follow the route taken by Drake's ships on the maps made by Mercator at the time; or to illustrate some phases of the Renaissance with a series of early printed books ! With this in view showcases were designed for the new library, and I hoped that leave would be given for books of special interest in the Fellows' Library regularly to be exhibited in them.

Meanwhile, however, Oldham became restive about certain gaps in my knowledge of the bindings. In particular, I had never seen the manuscripts and could tell him nothing about how they were bound. Under the stimulus of his inquiries, I approached the Fellows' Librarian. The safe where the manuscripts were kept was not in the gallery, but in the Warden's bedroom. This was indeed the *penetralia* of the Warden's Lodgings, and it had already a legendary reputation with me, since not so many years before a knowledgeable visitor who had made his way into it had recognized, in the bedside mat, a magnificent piece of Tudor tapestry; one section indeed of that Tapestry of the Roses which is now permanently kept in Thurbern's Chantry, and which is itself of some Arthurian interest. For it is decorated with the arms of Arthur's ancestor, Belinus, three crowns *or* on a field *azure*, and was probably woven for the occasion of the christening of Prince Arthur, Henry VII's eldest son, in Winchester Cathedral.

Accordingly, when at last I approached the safe with the key in my hands, it was with some excitement. I slid aside the metal grille, and was dashed to see at a glance that on the twenty or thirty manuscripts not a single medieval binding remained. Some were recent—one or two by Katherine Adams for example; a number, which were already in a somewhat sorry state, had been uniformly bound, perhaps about 1800, in a thin red leather, almost a skiver, numbered but not titled, and the covers in most instances already separating from the spines. It was a disappointment. But one did not get a chance every day to handle medieval books, so I pulled them out one by one and ran through one after another, catching a glimpse of an illumination here, or an interesting-looking text there, but making no systematic observations or notes. Two or three which were not in Latin but were in English caught my eye. One was very fat, some 480 leaves, paper not vellum, the text prose not verse, clearly about King Arthur and his Knights, but lacking a beginning or an end. Be it admitted to my shame that I had never read Malory, and my knowledge of him was about as sketchy as my knowledge of most things has alas had to remain. But I made a vague mental note of this prose Arthurian manuscript, and passed on to the next item.

It was a fantastic piece of good fortune that, some weeks later, I had to set out an exhibition in Moberly Library for the visit of a party from the Friends of the National Libraries. This was in the early days of the Friends, and Sir Frederic Kenyon, who was a Fellow of Winchester, had invited them down for the afternoon. We had no Caxton, but we had several fine Wynkyn de Wordes, one of them printed in 1496 and with the Caxton woodcut printer's device which Wynkyn de Worde took over from him. So it became necessary to 'get up' Caxton in order to write a sensible label for the exhibit, and naturally I went to Gordon Duff's article in the *Cambridge History of English Literature*, 'The Introduction of Printing into England and the Early Work of the Press.' In this article I came across a sentence which made my heart miss a beat.

'The compilation of the *Morte d'Arthur*', writes Duff, 'was finished in 1469, but of the compiler little is known save the name. He is generally believed to be the Sir Thomas Malory of Newbold Revell in Warwickshire who died in 1471.' And there then followed the phrases that excited me: 'No manuscript of the work is known, and though Caxton certainly revised it, exactly to what extent has never been settled.'

Was it possible that in the Warden's bedroom there was a manuscript of Malory? I went to Wells's bookshop in College Street and bought the Everyman text; the spelling modernized, but otherwise a verbal reprint of Caxton. I sought out the Librarian of the Fellows' Library and begged from him the key of the safe again, saying (what was indeed true) that there was some point I wished to check. With the Everyman edition beside the manuscript, it was apparent in a moment that this indeed was Malory, the text of the manuscript beginning in the middle of page 18 of the first volume in that edition. A brief examination showed that several of the colophons to individual sections had been shortened or eliminated by Caxton; and then I came across the startling evidence of revision in Book V, in which the robust archaisms of the author, following closely an older narrative in alliterative verse, had evidently been little to the liking of his editor and publisher.

Since that time I have learnt one or two of the elementary lessons of the tactics to be pursued in such circumstances. Lesson Number One is, of course, to be uncommunicative until one is fairly sure of at least some of the facts. But in my innocence I then only thought that this made a rather specially interesting exhibit for the Friends of the National Libraries. So indeed it did. But H. D. Ziman was at that time Secretary. When he saw it, he said he must write a column for the *Telegraph* next day. He wrote it—and a day or two later Professor Vinaver, who had been working already for some years on a new text of Malory and had of course an unrivalled knowledge of Malory's French sources and therefore an unrivalled equipment as Malory's editor, appeared from Manchester on my doorstep, asking to see the book. By this time I was thoroughly bewildered by the stir that the *Telegraph* paragraphs had caused. The book was not mine, nor did it even belong to the library of which I had charge. So I took him down to see it in the showcase, but refused to do more for him till I had instructions from the Warden and Fellows. This may have been in fact not unreasonable. One did not lightly risk a broadside from Sir Frederic Kenyon. But it must have seemed uncommonly churlish to a man who had made Malory already his life's work.

Kenyon pressed me strongly to produce an edition of the text. He had an intense belief in what he called 'discoverer's rights'. But I soon decided that this made very little sense, seeing that Vinaver had already the background which I should have to begin to acquire. I skimmed the cream quite unscrupulously in an article for *The Times*, in which the evidence of the new colophons was used to confirm the hypothesis already put forward by Kittredge, Vinaver, and others, that the *Morte Darthur* carried indications of having been written in prison—and so might with additional plausibility be attributed to that particular Malory who was known to have spent some time in prison; and in which I summarized the new impression that could be gained from the manuscript of Caxton's editorial activities, and in particular of his revision of Book V. This was followed by an article in the *Literary Supplement* in which I established (at least to my own satisfaction: Vinaver maintained perhaps rightly that though my conclusion was correct I had not adequately proved it) that the manuscript and Caxton's text were both descended not from Malory's autograph but from some intermediate copy which already contained a number of mistakes.

One thing however gave special satisfaction. I had the now famous colophon to Book IV, with its hitherto unknown reference to Malory as a 'Knight prisoner', photographed, and sent a print to Professor Kittredge of Harvard. He wrote this in reply:

Sept. 28/34

Dear Mr. Oakeshott,

Your most interesting letter and the facsimiles were forwarded to me from our American Cambridge in due order. Nothing that has crossed my path of late, has stirred me so deeply. The colophon, with its spelling of Malory's name, and its 'prisoner', is like a voice from the great deeps. One makes so many absurd guesses in this game of scholarship that it is reassuring to have one's theories substantiated by documentary evidence.

Accept my warmest thanks for your kindness and believe me

Yours sincerely,

G. L. KITTREDGE.

We are told that Saul the son of Kish went out to seek his father's asses and found a kingdom. The fate of the literary detective is comparable only in that, if he finds anything at all, he will find something different from that for which he is looking. It is seldom a kingdom. It is often a mare's nest. The asses almost always prove obstinately elusive. Certainly I did not, on this occasion, find them. All I could tell Oldham was that there were no bindings on the manuscripts to interest him.

There is no reason to think that the Winchester manuscripts were less accessible than other similar collections. That great scholar, M. R. James, had the Malory in his hands more than once before I saw it; it was a piece of singular good fortune for me that its importance did not happen to strike him. The catalogue made of the Fellows' Library in the early nineteenth century has a detailed and precise account of the book. It does not, however, mention Malory's name, but describes the manuscript by reference to the pages in the 1634 edition of the *Most Ancient and Famous History of Prince Arthur*, of which there was also a copy in the library. If Malory's name had been recorded in the catalogue, the manuscript could hardly have escaped notice so long. The moral seems to be that there are chances for the humblest gleaner even when the harvest has been reaped by experienced hands.

2

The English Prose *Morte*

C. S. LEWIS

I BEGIN by considering certain paradoxes which have been thrown up by the remarkable discoveries made in the last fifty years about Malory and the book (or books) which he translated, with modifications, from the French and which Caxton printed in 1485. They are five in number.

I. The work has long passed for a mirror of honour and virtue; the author appears to have been little better than a criminal.

II. The work strikes every reader as a rich feast of marvels, a tale 'of faerie damsels met in forest wide'; but a comparison of it with its sources seems to show Malory almost everywhere labouring to eliminate the marvellous and introduce the humdrum.

III. The work seems to many of us the typical specimen (because it is the first specimen we met) of Interwoven or Polyphonic narrative. But once again, comparison with the sources shows everything proceeding as if Malory detested this technique and did his best to pluck the threads apart.

IV. Its handling of the Grail story sounds deeply religious, and we have the sense that it is somehow profoundly connected with the final tragedy. But a case can be made out for the view that Malory evaded the religious significance and ignored or severed the connexion.

V. Malory seemed to Saintsbury (and doubtless to many) the man who alone 'makes of this vast assemblage of stories one story and one book'. The evidence of the Winchester MS. convinces Professor Vinaver that he really wrote several works which were never intended to form a whole.

If all these Paradoxes stand, they build up into a single grand Paradox. It is not of course paradoxical that a man's work should be other than he intended. What is paradoxical is that a man's work should succeed by its failure to realize every single intention he had when he made it. For it is as a mirror of honour, as a feast of marvels, as a Polyphonic narrative, as a romance of chivalry haunted by the higher mystery of the Grail, and as (in some sort) a unity, that the *Morte Darthur* has pleased. And not only pleased, but so far outstripped its rivals that it alone of all medieval prose romances has survived as a living book into our own century. In Malory's case, apparently, nothing succeeds like failure.

The reader should be warned at once that I am not attempting a *reductio ad absurdum*. I am not sure whether all the Paradoxes, in their sharpest form, will stand; but neither am I sure that all of them will completely fall. It therefore may be true that something like this paradoxical 'success by failure' has actually happened. If it has, then I want to draw a conclusion from it. But that will come later; in the meantime I will proceed to examine the five Paradoxes one by one.

I. The apparent discrepancy between the man and the work has seemed to some so formidable that they seek refuge in the possibility that the wicked Malory of the records is not our author but another man of the same name. But this is rather a desperate expedient. By all sound methodological principles a Malory whose Christian name was Thomas, who was a knight, who lived at the right time, and who was sometimes (like our Malory) in prison, must be assumed to be the author until any evidence to the contrary turns up. A far more respectable alternative is Professor Vinaver's view that the discrepancy is an illusion because the book (or books) are not in fact noble; the common belief in their 'morality' is based mainly on Caxton's preface.[1]

Yet I cannot quite accept this. It must of course be admitted that there are in the text untransmuted lumps of barbarism, like Arthur's massacre of the children (*C* I.27).

[1] *The Works of Thomas Malory*, ed. E. Vinaver (Oxford 1947), p. xxi. [In references to Malory in this volume *W* denotes this edition and *C* that of Caxton. Numbers refer to Book and chapter of *C* and to page, or page and line, of *W*.—Ed.]

And even when we discount these, no one can claim (or should demand) that the general tone conforms to the standards either of the New Testament or of modern, peace-time respectability. But I find in it, sometimes implicit, sometimes explicit, an unforced reverence not only for courage (that of course) but for mercy, humility, graciousness, and good faith. The best way to see it is to compare Malory's heroes, the characters he obviously admired, with those of Homer, Virgil, Renaissance drama, or even our earlier novelists. I cannot conceive that even the best of them—even Hector, Pallas, Othello, or Tom Jones—could ever have been made to understand why Lancelot wept like a beaten child after he had healed Sir Urry (*C* XIX. 12). A character from Corneille might understand the scene when Gawain, unhorsed, bids Marhaus to dismount, 'or else I will slay thy horse', and Marhaus, instantly obeying, replies, 'Grammercy, of your gentleness ye teach me courtesy' (*C* IV. 18); I doubt if he could equally have understood Lancelot's unresponsive endurance of Gawain's challenges (*C* XX. 20). I cannot deny either 'morality' (it is not a word I love) or something better to the imagination that shows us Lancelot refusing to take Gareth's victory from him at the tournament (*C* VII. 28), or Pelleas laying his sword across the throats of Gawain and Ettard (*C* IV. 22), or all Lancelot's contrition in Book XV, or the last message of Galahad, now almost a blessed spirit, to his father (*C* XVII. 22), or the final lament of Ector (*C* XXI. 13). In such passages, and indeed almost everywhere, we meet something which I chiefly hesitate to call 'morality' because it is so little like a code of rules. It is rather the civilization of the heart (by no means of the head), a fineness and sensitivity, a voluntary rejection of all the uglier and more vulgar impulses. We can describe it only in words derived from its own age, words which will now perhaps be mocked, such as *courtesy*, *gentleness*, *chivalry*. It makes the *Morte* a 'noble' as well as a 'joyous' history. I at any rate will never blacken the book to make it match the man.

But was the man so black? At first sight it would seem hard to deny, for he was convicted of cattle-lifting, poaching, extortion, sacrilegious robbery, attempted murder, and rape.

The record suggests to Professor Vinaver a man who at the age of forty 'from being a peaceable and presumably well-to-do citizen . . . became a law-breaker'.[1] And if we apply certain habitual conceptions of our own to Malory's record, this result seems inevitable. But are these conceptions possibly too local and modern? 'Citizen', 'law-breaker', and (why has that come in?) 'well-to-do'. I suspect that a man of Malory's class and time would not much have relished the titles 'peaceable' or 'citizen'; and the real question about his actions probably was for him, and should be for us, not whether they broke the law but whether they were cowardly, discourteous, treacherous, and (in a word) unknightly. It is not clear that they need have been. Our record of them comes from lawyers. In that age evidence was not scientifically sifted and accusers laid it on thick. In every county civil war exploited, and was exploited by, local feuds. Legal proceedings, whether civil or criminal, were often primarily moves in family quarrels. We need not assume that he did all the things he was accused of. But even if he did, he need not have been, by all standards, a villain. Cattle-lifting was a gentlemanly crime. If he killed other men's deer, so did the Douglas at Otterburn. A knightly ambush and encounter could be attempted murder. Rape need mean no more than abduction; from the legal point of view Lancelot committed rape when he saved Guinevere from the fire. If Malory, loving Joan Smyth *par amours*, and knowing her cuckoldy knave of a husband to be little better than a King Mark, carried her off behind him at 'a great wallop' and perhaps thus saved her from a broken head and two black eyes at home, he may have done what a good knight and a true lover ('of a sinful man') should. That he often fell below the highest standards of chivalry, we may well believe; we need not believe that he fell flagrantly below them. He might, on the evidence, have been as good a knight as Tristram; for what should we think of Tristram himself if our knowledge of him were derived only from King Mark's solicitors?

Of course this picture is conjectural; but it is equally conjecture to represent him, on the strength of the records,

[1] Op. cit. p. xvi.

as the sort of man who in our days becomes a 'criminal'. We don't know what he was really like, and I suppose we never shall.

II. This Paradox, like the next two, of course involves the assumption that differences between Malory's text and the extant MSS. of his originals are due to Malory. I think this is very probably so. I agree with Professor Vinaver that it is monstrous to set out by assuming that Malory had no spark of originality and therefore to trace everything in which he differs from those MSS. to a hypothetical, lost, intermediary. But probability is not certainty. We cannot be absolutely sure that any given passage, peculiar to Malory, or even any given omission, was his own. Everything I say about Paradoxes II, III, and IV must be understood with this *caveat*.

There are fewer marvels in Malory than in the corresponding French romances. There are, to be sure, at least two places where he introduces a marvel which they lack. But one of these seems to me[1] to be almost certainly the (not unhappy) result of a graphic error. In *C* XVII. 19 the *sword* 'arose great and marvellous and was full of great heat that many men fell for dread'. In the French it was a wind (*ung vent*) that so arose. I suppose that either Malory or the scribe of the French MS. he was using, having the sword in his head from the preceding passage, wrote it here, intending to write *wind*. The other is in *C* IV. 6, where a sudden, presumably miraculous light of torches in Malory replaces the French text's ordinary arrival of torches carried by ladies. But this, or both these, amount to nothing against the opposite instances. No one disputes that Malory's text naturalizes, negatively, by the omission of wonders, and positively, by introducing practical, mundane details. When Arthur defeats Damas he makes proper legal arrangements for the righting of the wrongs Damas has done: 'I will that ye give unto your brother all the whole manor with the appurtenance, under this form, that Sir Ontzlake hold the manor of you, and yearly to give you a palfrey' (*C* IV. 12). Similarly (in *C* VII. 35) the defeated knights swear homage and

[1] Vinaver (op. cit. p. 1569 n. on 1027, 30–32) prefers a different explanation.

fealty to Gareth 'to hold of him for evermore'. King Anguysh sending Marhaus to Cornwall, assures him that his expenses will be amply covered (*C* VIII. 4). When Tristram bleeds over the lady's bed in *C* VIII. 14, we are told the extent of damage almost as if Malory had made up the laundry list—'both the over-sheet and the nether-sheet and the pillows and the head-sheet'. Mordred explains at length, and very sensibly, why young knights are at a disadvantage on horseback (*C* IX. 4). Lancelot's habit of talking in his sleep is noted (*C* XI. 8). Best of all, we are told exactly how much it had cost the Queen (£20,000) to send out knights in search of him (*C* XII. 9).

The Paradox here is not very strong, for it turns on the contrast between Malory's supposed intentions and the known effect of his work. For, clearly, even if we know what he did, we can only guess what he intended. It is possible to imagine a burly, commonsensible man who was always trying to turn the faerie world of the romances into something much more earthy and realistic. Accepting that picture, we may smile at the 'success by failure', the happy frustration of his vain labour which has made his book for centuries the chief delight of all who love 'the fairy way of writing'. But a quite different picture is equally possible. If you write fairy-tales and receive letters from your child readers, you will find that children are always asking the sort of questions that Malory is always answering. A simple and serious delight in marvellous narrative most emphatically does not involve any indifference to mundane details. The more seriously you take the story the more you want to tie everything up and to know how people got from one place to another, and what they had to eat, and how all outstanding issues were settled. Neglect of these points, whether in writer or reader, means that the whole thing is merely conventional or playful. Multiplication of marvels goes with the same attitude. Those who love them, as alone they can be loved, for their suggestiveness, their quality, will not increase their number. Two enchanters, two ghosts, two ferlies are always half as impressive as one. Every supposedly naturalistic change that Malory made in the story might proceed from a far fuller belief and a more profound delight in it than the French authors had ever known. He would not be the less English for that.

Once more, I ask no one to choose between these two pictures. Either, as it seems to me, will fit the facts. We shall never know which is true.

III. The excellent remarks of Professor Vinaver on what I have called Interwoven or Polyphonic narrative[1] will have made it clear to all readers that this is a real technique, not, as an earlier generation supposed, a mere muddle or an accidental by-product of conflation. It is a technique not peculiar to medieval prose romance. We find it fully developed over long stretches of Ovid's *Metamorphoses*. The rudiments of it are there in parts of *Beowulf*. The epic poets of Italy took it over from the romance, and Spenser took it over from them. Sidney re-wrote the *Arcadia* to make it more polyphonic. Milton seems to have toyed with the idea of using it for a great epic; he certainly acknowledged that to depart from Aristotelian unity in a narrative might be an enriching of art.[2]

Quite clearly the method continued to be used for centuries, not in blind obedience to tradition but because it gave pleasure. Dante selected this feature of chivalrous romance for special praise: *Arturi regis ambages pulcerrime*.[3] Tasso confesses that all knights and ladies prefer it; everyone reads Ariosto, and no one reads Trissino.[4] He even records how his father discovered by sad experience that 'unity of action gave little pleasure'.[5] The vogue of the Polyphonic in fact lasted longer than that of the modern novelistic technique has yet done. It would be interesting to analyse, and perhaps not difficult to account for, the pleasure it gave. But that would be too long a digression. What matters for the moment is that it did please and can please still. To the present day no one enjoys Malory's book who does not enjoy its *ambages*, its interweaving.

For it is certainly interwoven. Arthur has a war against five kings. To repair his losses he must make new knights. His selection sends Bagdemagus, malcontent, from the

[1] Op. cit. pp. xlviii–liii. [2] *Reason of Church Government*, Pref. Bk. II.
[3] *De Vulgari Eloquentia*, I. x. 2. [4] *Discorsi Poetici*, II.
[5] *Apologia in difesa alla Ger.Lib.*

court, and the story of his wanderings crosses the latter end of Merlin's story. Arthur meanwhile has got involved in the affairs of Damas and Ontzlake, which in their turn involve both him and Accolon in the machinations of Morgan, which lead to the banishment of her son Uwain, which leads to his joint errantry with Gawain, which brings them both (now in company with Marhaus) to those three damsels at the river-head who fork the story into three (*C* IV. 4–19) . . . and so on. Those who dislike this sort of thing will not much like Malory.

Yet it may be, as Professor Vinaver concludes,[1] that Malory 'strongly disliked' it himself. Certainly the evidence that he constantly simplified is irresistible. Whether he wanted to simplify still further and get rid of the Polyphonic altogether, or whether he wanted to go just as far as he has gone and liked the degree of Polyphony which survives under his treatment, we do not know. If he wanted to get rid of it altogether, he has undoubtedly failed. To anyone who comes to his work fresh from modern literature its Polyphonic character will be at first one of the most noticeable things about it. And the work will be liked, where it is liked, not despite of this peculiarity but (in part) because of it.

IV. This Paradox involves us in two subjects: Malory's treatment of the holy quest, and the connexion, if any, between it and other matters in his text.

Professor Vinaver's view on the first subject depends on the interpretation of a great many different passages. I shall refer to them both by the Book and Chapter of Caxton's edition and by the page and line of the Professor's (which I indicate by the letter *W*). They fall into four classes.

1. A passage[2] held to indicate Malory's 'confidence in the unfailing merits of Arthurian chivalry' (*W* 1524). This is *C* XVI. 3 (*W* 946.18) where a Hermit in the French text condemns the Round Table for *luxure* and *orgueil*; but in Malory, for 'sin and wickedness'. I cannot myself see that the substitution of the general for the particular makes the condemnation less severe.

[1] Op. cit. p. lii.

[2] At least I think this must be the passage Vinaver has in mind on p. 1524.

2. Passages where Malory substitutes the worldly for the religious. Thus in *C* xvi. 3 (*W* 945.10) the dying Uwain in the French asks that prayer be made for his soul; in Malory he asks to be remembered to Arthur and the court, 'and for old brotherhood, think on me'. (This phrase itself might imply a request for prayers, but I would not press that.) Again, in *C* xvi. 6 (*W* 955.9) Bors, surprisingly, and without authority from the French, says that he who achieves the Grail will win 'much earthly worship'. Both these, and especially the latter, are strong evidence for Professor Vinaver's view: if it is felt that they are sufficient to colour the whole narrative, then that view will be unassailable. Two other passages which might be quoted here seem to me, on the other hand, to rank as 'worldly' only if we adopt standards of worldliness which are almost intolerably severe. In *C* xiii. 19 (*W* 896.11) Malory allows the contrite Lancelot to be 'somewhat comforted' when day breaks and he hears the birds sing. In the French (which is finely imagined) the morning and the birds directly produce the conviction of God's anger, which in Malory comes home to Lancelot only when he realizes that he has lost his horse and his armour. This is certainly very practical, homely, English, and (in a word) Malorian; but it does not for me empty the scene of all religious significance. Again in *C* xvii. 13 (*W* 1011.31–1012.1) Malory's Lancelot (not his French equivalent) after a month of fasting on board ship with no one but a dead lady for company, 'was somewhat weary of the ship' and went ashore 'to play him'. (Middle English *play* in such a context is of course a very mild word; we should have said 'to stretch his legs' or 'to relax'.) Now I think a man might have done that and yet be a very good sort of penitent on the whole. Both passages, indeed, are for me specimens of that Malorian realism which brings the story to life; they make Lancelot, not a stained-glass figure, but a real man, though a contrite one.[1] It is proper, however, to point out that the difference between Professor Vinaver and myself may be simply the same difference there was between the French originals and Malory, the difference between the hard lines and rigid

[1] [Cf. pp. 87, 92 below.—Ed.]

schematization of Latin thought, and the softening, compromising temper of us islanders. (For some say our best Christians are all Pelagians, and our best atheists all Puritans, at heart.)

3. The third class is, for me, the hardest to feel sure about. In *C* XIII. 14 (*W* 886.18) the qualification for success in the holy quest is, in the French, *chevaillierie celestiale*; in the English, 'virtuous living'. In *C* XIII. 16 (*W* 891.32) it is again, for Malory, 'knightly deeds and virtuous living'; for the French author it is service to the Creator, defence of Holy Church, and the offering to Christ of the treasure (one's soul) which has been entrusted to one. In *C* XVI. 6 (*W* 956.2) Bors is praised in the French for his 'religious', in Malory for his 'stable', life. In *C* XVI. 13 (*W* 968.11) Lionel is condemned by the French author because *n'a an soi nule vertu de Nostre Seignor qui en estant le tiegne*; by Malory, because 'he is a murderer and doth contrary to the order of knighthood'. These are I think the strongest specimens. That in *C* XV. 5 (*W* 931.25) seems to me weak. It is true that the motive which Malory gives Lancelot for joining in a certain fray is, as Professor Vinaver claims, incongruous with the Quest; but then Malory is fully aware of this and in the very next chapter (*C* XV. 6; *W* 933.32–934.4) makes his recluse tell Lancelot that such 'bobaunce and pride of the world' must be abandoned. The insertion of both these passages by Malory would seem to emphasize the very point which, it is claimed, he was ignoring. We might perhaps add *C* XVI. 17 (*W* 974.15–17) where the edifying mutual forgiveness of Bors and his brother is also peculiar to Malory.

But the earlier passages remain, and I will not for a moment dispute that they all indicate an important change made by Malory and affecting his version throughout. The question is how we are to define it. At first sight I am tempted to say that where the originals used specifically religious, Malory uses ethical, concepts: *virtuous* for *celestial*, *knightly* and *virtuous* for the offering of the heart to Christ, *stable* for *religious*. This certainly means that the choice before Malory's knights is not that between 'religion' in the technical sense and active life in the world. They are to go on being knights (*C* XIII. 20; *W* 899.1–5); just as the soldiers who came to the Baptist were told to go on being soldiers.[1] Malory in fact holds the same view as Langland and Gower and many other English medieval moralists. No man need leave the Order to which he has been called, but every man must begin really to fulfil the functions for which that Order exists. The recall is not from knighthood to the cloister, but from knighthood as it has come to be (full of 'sin and wickedness') to knighthood as it was intended to be, grounded in 'patience and humility' (*C* XVI. 3; *W* 945–7). Admittedly, then, the story is ethical, as against mystical. But we must not say 'ethical, as against religious', for the ethical claim and the attempted ethical response, when prompted by a vision, purged by confession and penance, supported and corrected at every turn by voices, miracles, and spiritual counsels, is precisely the religious as it most commonly appears in secular vocations. And *stability* (perseverance to the end, or consistency) is of course essential.

4. Finally, we have those passages which exalt the supremacy of Lancelot over all other knights. There may be some difference of opinion as to which we should include in this class. I certainly would not include *C* XVII. 22 (*W* 1035.11–12) where Galahad, almost at the threshold of Heaven, sends to his father a message bidding him 'remember of this unstable world'. The words are full of knightly courtesy, filial duty, and Christian charity, but of course they are a warning and (by delicatest implication) a reproof. It is Galahad whom they exalt. Nor do I find much 'rehabilitation' of Lancelot in Malory's insertion at the end of *C* XVII. 23 (*W* 1036.19–1037.7). Lancelot does not relate the adventures of the Grail *simpliciter*, but those 'that he had seen'. Bors had seen, and Bors told, what Lancelot had not seen. One would expect the surviving knights each to contribute to the report which Arthur naturally demanded. And the passage repeats Galahad's message, with its grave implication. Another doubtful place is *C* XVI. 1 (*W* 941.20–22). Here Gawain says that 'if one thing were not' (surely beyond all doubt the 'one thing' is his adultery?) Lancelot would be matchless. But as things are, far from

[1] Luke iii. 14.

rising (for purposes of this Quest) to the level of Galahad, Perceval, and Bors, Lancelot 'is as we be', is just like the rest of us, *nous autres*, Ectors and Gawains—'but if he take the more pain on him'.[1] I cannot imagine a better way of making us feel how Lancelot has sunk than thus to let us hear lesser men exclaiming that at last he's no better than they.

The passages on which the Vinaverian view must finally rest are those where Malory deliberately inserts the praise of Lancelot. A damsel in *C* XIII. 5 (*W* 863.30), a hermit in *C* XV. 4 (*W* 930.14), and a second hermit in *C* XVI. 5 (*W* 948.27–8) all remind us that Lancelot was the best knight, for a sinful man, that ever lived. The reservation is of course important; but in spite of it, I am prepared to admit that all these passages may be meant to blunt for us the edge of the abasement which Lancelot undergoes in the French text. But it also seems to me equally possible that they were intended to have—and for me they have—a very different effect. It is a question of what may be called the logic of the imagination. If one wanted to exhibit in a novel the theme that intellectual achievements were no passport to heaven, one would not choose for one's protagonist some mediocrity who has 'got a good second'. Only a fool would labour to show the failure, on the highest level, of pretensions which were doubtfully adequate even on their own. Obviously one would build one's protagonist up to the stature of a Porson, a Sherrington, or a Mahaffy. If you want to show that one sort of achievement is inferior to, even incommensurable with, another, then of course the more splendid (in its own kind) your specimen is, the more impressive its failure (in another kind) will be. Every word said in praise of Lancelot as a good knight 'of a sinful man'—as the bravest, most courteous, most faithful in his love, but not seriously hitherto attempting that perfection of chastity and all other virtues which the Christian law demands of the knight, in his own fashion, no less than of the contemplative —serves all the more to drive home the moral of the whole story, makes it all the clearer that with the Quest we have

[1] I don't believe this means 'even though he takes'. Rather 'unless he were to take'; i.e. he is (and will remain) like us unless he should take more pains than he's taking at present. [Cf. p. 88 below.—Ed.]

entered a region where even what is best and greatest by the common standards of the world 'falls into abatement and low price'.

But, as before, I end in uncertainty. I am sure that Malory's handling has not on me the effect, and therefore need not have been meant to have the effect, which Professor Vinaver supposes. I know it has the opposite effect on me. I cannot rule out the possibility that it was intended to have this opposite effect. I do not claim to know that it was.

So much for his treatment of the Quest. As regards its relation to other parts of his work, I feel a little more confident. It appears to me to be unmistakably linked with the *Morte*. Before the Quest begins, before Galahad is begotten, when the Grail first appears before Lancelot in the house of Pelles, Malory inserts the prophecy that 'when this rich thing goeth about, the Round Table shall be broken for a season'. (*C* XI. 2; *W* 793.32–36). I do not know what to make of 'for a season', and how right (as often) Caxton was to omit it! But it is Malory who has introduced, even if Caxton perfected, the note of doom: the dreadful hint that the best is fatal to the good. Then in the Quest itself (*C* XIII. 20; *W* 897.27–28) Lancelot promises 'by the faith of his body' never to come in Guinevere's 'fellowship' again if he can avoid it. Then, when the Quest is over, almost immediately, Lancelot 'forgat the promise and the perfection that he made in the Quest'. This is in the French; but as if this were not enough Malory must add that this was the inadequately repented 'bosom-sin' which had led him to fail in that attempt (*C* XVIII. 1; *W* 1045.12–16). Notice too that in thus forgetting his promise Lancelot is verifying the diagnosis ('not stable, but . . . likely to turn again') made upon him by the hermit in *C* XVI 5.—a passage, so far as we know, of Malory's own making. The connexion here, if unintended, is singularly fortunate. But Malory still feels he has not done enough. Returning to *C* XVIII. 1, we find a dialogue between Lancelot and Guinevere inserted (*W* 1045.30–1048.14) in which he almost begs the terrible woman to release him, pleading, 'I was but late in the quest,' confessing that 'privy thoughts to return to your love' were the lime-twigs he could not escape, trying to make her understand that such experiences 'may not be lightly forgotten'. Then later (*C* xix. 10–12) we have what is perhaps the greatest of all passages peculiar to Malory, the healing of Sir Urry. Here Lancelot is proved by infallible signs to be in one sense (he knows too well in what and how limited a sense) the best knight of the world. Hence, while all praise him to the skies, he can only weep like a beaten child. As he failed on the Quest, so (for the same reason) he is failing now. In him, its highest specimen, the whole Round Table is failing; on it and him, as the result of his illicit love, the prophecies begin to be fulfilled. They are, no doubt, worked out through a tangle of human motives, the spite of Agravain and Mordred, the assumption of the blood-feud by Gawain. Of course. The fulfilment of the prophecies about Oedipus came about through seemingly free agents obeying human motives. That is how prophecies are fulfilled in good stories; no one ever suggested that the motivation somehow abolishes the connexion between the prediction and the event. And when all is nearly over and the doom worked out, Lancelot again recalls to us the source of the whole tragedy: 'For in the quest of the Sangreal I had forsaken the vanities of the world had not your love been' (*C* xxi. 9; *W* 1253.14–15).

And still, though I cannot see how any reader fails to see the connexion, I cannot be certain whether Malory himself saw it or not.

V. Finally, did Malory write one book or eight? Close study of the Winchester MS. has convinced Professor Vinaver that he wrote eight; instead of the *Morte Darthur* we have the 'Works' of Malory, and inconsistencies between them no longer matter—indeed, no longer exist, for independent worlds of invention cannot be inconsistent with one another. This view has been seriously criticized by Mr. D. S. Brewer.[1] He points out that the eight 'works' are full of backward and forward references, their order not alterable, and 'bridge' passages often supplied. I think I should be on Mr. Brewer's side in this question, if I were

[1] ['Form in the Morte Darthur.' *Medium Ævum* xxi (1952), pp. 14–24. The argument is restated in Mr. Brewer's essay in the present volume.—Ed.]

not bogged down in a preliminary doubt as to what precisely the question is.

I believe I know fairly well what we mean if we say, '*Pickwick* is one work, but *Pickwick* and *Great Expectations* are two works'. We mean that within *Pickwick*, as within *Great Expectations*, there are characters that continue or recur, and that there are causal connexions, and the later parts presuppose the earlier; whereas there are no common characters and no causal connexions shared by both. But ask me the same questions about *Barchester Towers* and *The Last Chronicle*; already a shade of ambiguity has crept in. Now go a step further. What of *Paradise Lost* and *Paradise Regained*? Here there are characters common to both, and the later poem presupposes and recalls events in the earlier. Satan's temptation of Christ presupposes his rebellion against God and his expulsion from Heaven. And if Satan, and the whole story, were as purely Milton's invention as Archdeacon Grantly is Trollope's, the two poems would stand in the same not very easily defined relation as the two novels. Actually, however, Satan's career with all its causal and chronological structure already exists in the Fathers and in popular belief, before Milton sets pen to paper, and continues to exist whether he wants us to treat *Regained* as a sequel or as a wholly separate poem. Presupposals of events in *Paradise Lost*, and backward references, are bound to occur. It may be impossible to say whether a given instance of them illustrates the unity of the two poems or whether it merely exhibits at one point the external, pre-existing, non-Miltonic unity of the matter he worked on. Hence we may generalize: wherever there is a matter (historical or legendary) previous and external to the author's activity, the question, 'One work or many?' loses a good deal of its meaning. And of course Malory's matter was of this kind.

On top of this a special difficulty arises from the fact that Malory was a medieval author. If it were possible to question him directly, in what form should we put our question? It would be no use asking him how many books he thought he had written; he would think we meant the material volumes or 'quairs'. If we asked him, 'How many tales?' he might enumerate more than eight. Such expressions as 'Thus endeth the tale of . . .' (*C* II. 19; *W* 92.22), or 'the adventure of' (*C* III. 8; *W* 108.28) or 'the quest of' (*C* III. 11; *W* 113.34) occur within the Vinaverian units. If we talked to him about 'artistic unity', he would not understand. We might finally, in desperation, try to find out whether he was at all worried at the appearance in one passage of some knight whose death had been recorded in an earlier passage. He would, I feel certain, simply refer us to 'the French book' as his authority. For the difficulty between Malory and us would not be merely linguistic. We should by the very form of our questions be presupposing concepts his mind was not furnished with. Did any Middle English author conceive clearly that he was writing fiction, a single work of fiction, which should obey the laws of its own inner unity but need not cohere with anything else in the world? I cannot believe it. They are all, even Chaucer, handing on, embellishing, expanding, or abridging a matter received from some source. They feel free to illuminate it at any number of points with their own vivid imagination, and even to correct what seems to them improbable, improper, or unedifying. But whatever their own degree of actual belief or of scepticism (were they clearly aware of either? did they for the most part even raise such questions?) they all proceed as if they were more or less historians; unscholarly, decorating, and emotional historians to be sure, like Livy or Plutarch, but (by and large) historians still. I do not for a moment believe that Malory had any intention either of writing a single 'work' or of writing many 'works' as we should understand the expressions. He was telling us about Arthur and the knights. Of course his matter was one—the same king, the same court. Of course his matter was many—they had had many adventures.

The choice we try to force upon Malory is really a choice for us. It is our imagination, not his, that makes the work one or eight or fifty. We can read it either way. We can read it now one way, now another. We partly make what we read.

As will be seen, the examination of all five Paradoxes produces in me varying degrees of doubt (weakest as regards the Third, strongest as regards the Second and Fifth) about Professor Vinaver's idea of Malory's intentions; but it produces no confidence in any alternative theory. The net result is that Malory eludes me. Perhaps, then, I shall be able to find him in his style, for they say that a man's style is himself. Unfortunately, Malory turns out to have not a style, but styles. The inverted and alliterative language of the Roman War has little likeness to the limpid, unobtrusive prose in which we follow the adventures of knights errant. And we know why. The one is from the Alliterative *Morte*, the other renders, and copies as closely as English can, the style of the French prose romances. In both, Malory writes such a style as he has most lately read. And we cannot say that this subjection to the model is a prentice weakness which he outgrew in his maturity. At the very end, as soon as the Stanzaic *Morte* comes before him, the tell-tale features, the tags, inversions, and alliterations, creep into his prose: 'while we thus in holes us hide'—'that was wary and wise'—'droop and dare'—'shred them down as sheep in a fold' (*C* xx. 19; *W* 1211–12). And when he leaves his originals altogether to reflect upon the story (*C* xviii. 25; *W* 1119–20), we have a style different from all these. There are more (ultimately) Latin derivatives close together (*constrain*, *divers*, *negligence*, *stability*, and *rasure*), and doublets like 'bring forth fruit and flourish', 'springeth and flourisheth', 'arase and deface', 'deface and lay apart'. This is quite unlike the prose used in his own (or what we take to be his own) additions to the narrative parts, especially those dialogues which he inserts more freely as he nears the end. These are no doubt admirable; but who, on purely internal evidence, could have picked them out (as almost anyone could pick out the alliterative passage about the dream in *C* v. 4)? They may be better than the surrounding prose which reproduces the French, but they are all of a piece with it. Malory's greatest original passages arise when he is most completely absorbed in the story and realizes the characters so fully that they begin to talk for him of their own accord; but they talk a language he has largely learned from his sources. The very ease with which he wanders away from this style into that of some inferior source or into a language of his own (which he may have thought 'higher') suggests that he hardly knows what he is doing. Thus, while in one sense it would be monstrous to say that he 'has no style' (he has written prose as musical, as forthright, as poignant, as was ever heard in England) it would be true in another. He has no style of his own, no characteristic manner. (If you were searching all literature for a man who might be described as 'the opposite of Pater', Malory would be a strong candidate.) In a style or styles so varied, everywhere so indebted to others, and perhaps most original precisely where it is most indebted, one cannot hopefully seek *l'homme même*. Here also Malory vanishes into a mist.

And this result neither surprises nor disappoints me. I have called this essay 'The English prose *Morte*', because I think we may deceive ourselves by such expressions as 'Malory's *Morte Darthur*' or 'The Works of Sir Thomas Malory'. They sound so dangerously like 'Browning's *Sordello*' or 'The Works of Jane Austen'. But there is no real parallel. Our familiar concept of 'author-and-his-book' is foiled by the composite works of the Middle Ages. Even in *Troilus and Criseyde*, where the whole is much shorter and the last worker's additions are much larger and known more certainly, we are foiled. We can sort out the Boccaccian and the Chaucerian passages. But not the Boccaccian and the Chaucerian element. For of course the surviving Boccaccio is modified by the interpolated Chaucer, and the Chaucer modified (this is less often stressed) by the Boccaccio. In the end we cannot really say that either author, nor even in what proportion each author, is responsible for the total effect. The prose *Morte* is very much more complicated. Whatever Malory's intentions—if he had any intentions—may have been, it is agreed on all hands that he has changed the tale very little. From the nature of the case he could not have changed it much. It is too vast, too filled with its own strong life, to be much affected by alterations so comparatively short and sporadic as his. This does not mean that his contribution is of negligible value. Like so many medieval authors (like, for example, the poet of *Cleanness* and *Patience*), at point after point he adds vividness, throws some figure into bolder relief, cuts away an excrescence, or sweetens some motive that he rightly found odious.[1] The process may be described as 'touching up'. But there is no question of a great artist giving to a pupil's work those strokes of genius 'which make all the difference'. Rather, a deft pupil has added touches here and there to a work which, in its majestic entirety, he could never have conceived; and from which his own skill has been chiefly learned. Though he has in fact improved it, it was (by our standards, not by those of the Middle Ages) rather cheek of him to try. But even if he had done harm, he would not have done much harm.

If some people find it distressing to have a work which cannot be assigned to any single author, let me remind them that in another art we are familiar with this sort of thing. I am thinking of a great cathedral, where Saxon, Norman, Gothic, Renaissance, and Georgian elements all co-exist, and all grow together into something strange and admirable which none of its successive builders intended or foresaw. Under Malory's work lies that of the French prose romancers; under theirs, that of Chrétien, Wace, and other poets; under that, Geoffrey, and perhaps the Breton *lais*; deepest of all, who knows what fragments of Celtic myth or actual British history? Malory is only the last of many restorers, improvers, demolitionists; if you will, of misunderstanders. Meanwhile, the great cathedral of words stands solidly before us and imposes on us a meaning which is largely independent of their varying and perhaps incompatible purposes. Who, if any, first saw or intended the tragic and ironic parallel between Mordred's begetting and Galahad's? Or the necessity that the Grail should bring not peace but a sword? Or the three-storied effect inevitably produced by the intermediate position of the good knights between the villains like Mark and the perfect knights like Percivale? Or the deep suggestiveness of Arthur's relation to that dark family (Morgan, Morgause, and the rest) from whom he emerges, who lie in wait for him, and who mysteriously return in his last hour to take him away?

I said just now that Malory was only the last of the makers

[1] e.g. at *C* VIII. 9 (*W* 385.6–8) where he turns Tristram from a cad into an ordinary amorous young man.

of the *Morte*. I should have said, last but one (or even last but two). It follows from the view I am trying to put that Caxton's text is not most usefully regarded as a corruption. He touched up Malory as Malory touched up his predecessors and by the same right. The greatest service that he did the old fabric was one of demolition. Most unluckily (and probably, as Professor Vinaver thinks, early in his career) Malory had come across the Alliterative *Morte*. It is not a first-class poem, not comparable in epic quality to the battle scenes of Layamon, and it treats the dullest and most incredible part of the whole Arthurian legend. It is far easier to suspend one's disbelief in enchantments than in vast contradictions of known history scrawled across a whole continent; and a narrative of unbroken military successes, dull even when true, is insufferable when feigned. It is defeat, or (as in the *Iliad*) discords within one of the armies, that we need for epic. Malory swallowed this poem almost whole, except that by separating it from the *Morte* he deprived it of the tragic close and the moral judgement[1] which had saved it from total paltriness. He also surrendered his style without resistance to the influence of the alliterative metre, which, degenerate even in the original, becomes in prose a noisy rumble. Caxton wisely abridged the whole dreary business, and removed (he might well have used the knife more boldly) some of the traces of the metre. Thus where Winchester's (and no doubt Malory's) text read

> Now fecche me, seyde sir Pryamus, my vyall that hangys by the gurdyll of my haynxman, for hit is full of the floure of the four good watyrs that passis from Paradyse, the mykill fruyte in fallys that at one day fede shall us all. . . .

Caxton gives

> And Priamus took from his page a vial full of the four waters that came out of Paradise.

Notice that Caxton has made it much more Malorian, more like the best and most typical parts of Malory, than Malory himself had done. This is 'forcing a man to be free', making him himself (*C* v. 10; *W* 234.11–14). Again in *C* v. 8 (*W*

[1] Alliterative *Morte* 3393–3402, ed. E. Brock (E.E.T.S. 1865).

219.16–17) we owe to Caxton 'the ground trembled and dindled' instead of 'all the vale dyndled'. The division into chapters, if sometimes unskilfully done, has made the book everywhere more readable. The rubrics he prefixed to the chapters have become as much part of its beauty as the glosses of the *Ancient Mariner's*. Sometimes, as in 'how Lancelot fell to his old love again', they direct us unerringly to the pith of what follows (*C* XVIII. 1); again and again they are evocative in the highest degree.

I am not of course suggesting that Caxton's share in the final effect is remotely comparable to Malory's; only that he too, in his degree, has helped a little, and that it is no misfortune if his text has counted for so much in the English imagination. That is why I have usually quoted not only from Caxton but even from Caxton edited by Pollard; the household book. I enjoy my cathedral as it has stood the test of time and demand no restoration. I have no more wish to discard Caxton for Malory than to discard Malory for the French romances.

It would distress me if anyone took this to imply the slightest depreciation of Professor Vinaver's great edition. It is an indispenable work of which English scholarship may well be proud, and my own debts to it will be obvious. Indeed the view I have taken allows me to give Professor Vinaver a place higher, in my opinion, than scholarship of itself could claim. I hesitated a while ago whether to call Malory last but one, or last but two, of the many who worked at the prose *Morte*. For has not Professor Vinaver some right to be numbered among them? He has not, naturally, allowed himself the liberties of a Malory or even of a Caxton. His chisel has touched no stone of the building. But he has made a new approach, and one which many modern pilgrims will find more congenial. His book smacks of our own century as Caxton's smacked of his. The division into eight romances, and above all the title, *The Works* of Malory, whether right or wrong (or neither), makes it far more digestible by contemporary critical conceptions than the old *Morte*. The *Works*, the Complete Works—that is what our libraries are used to. Already Malory fits more comfortably on the shelf beside the 'works' of everyone else.

And the mere look of the pages—the paragraphing and the inverted commas—acclimatizes the book still further. Beyond question, Professor Vinaver has shown the cathedral from a new angle; placed the modern pilgrim where he will enjoy it best. And now that his edition is deservedly reaching the stage of cheap reprints, it may in its turn become the household book; until perhaps *alter Achilles*, some second Vinaver (a little cold to the first one as he is a little cold to Caxton) recalls his generation to the long forgotten book of 1485 or even to the French, and someone like myself puts in a plea for what will then be the old, the traditional, 'Works of Malory'. And all these preferences will be legitimate and none of them 'right' or 'wrong'. The cathedral of words is so large that everyone can find in it the work of his favourite period; and here, as you could not do in a real cathedral, you can always strip that favourite work of later accretions without pulling the whole thing down. What you must not do is to call those bits 'the' or 'the real' cathedral. They might have been. The whole might have been designed by one man and finished in one style. But that is not what happened. Though every part of it was made by a man, the whole has rather grown than been made. Such things have a kind of existence that is almost midway between the works or art and those of nature.

3

On Art and Nature: A letter to C. S. Lewis

E. VINAVER

MY DEAR LEWIS,

Of all the contributors to this volume I am the most fortunate. You have shown me your essay and asked me to write a reply to it or, to quote your own words, 'a development from it'. The privilege is a perilous one, and at first I hesitated to take up the friendly challenge; but the prospect of a dialogue with you on the vital issues you have raised is irresistible.

Everything you say is enlightening and much of it is revealing. I have lived with Malory for many years and I think I know how he impresses me; but I would rather leave the reader with *your* impressions firmly fixed in his mind, for I consider them an acquisition for us all and not a matter for discussion. What might usefully be discussed is not what you feel about Malory, but the way in which you account for your feelings—your interpretation of your reaction to the book.

I find this interpretation debatable, and there you probably agree. You sum it up by saying: 'the net result is that Malory eludes me.' I confess that up to that point, as I went on reading your essay, the familiar but invariably fresh magic of your language and thought lulled me into a delightful state of acquiescence. But when I came to these words I had to pause. Surely, I reflected, if there is one critic whom Malory does *not* elude it is C. S. Lewis; hence, if the 'net result' of his argument is to make him deny so obvious a fact there must be something wrong with his argument. I did not, and I could not, ask myself *why* Malory 'eluded' you, because he quite clearly had not done so. The only question in my mind was why you *thought* he had eluded you. What was it that gave you the feeling that you were faced with something strange and 'paradoxical': not even with one paradox, but with as many as five? There is no simple and uniform answer to this question. But as I was looking for a possible answer a passage from *A Winter's Tale* came to my mind—the lines spoken by Polixenes in Act IV:

> You see, sweet maid, we marry
> A gentle scion to the wildest stock,
> And make conceive a bark of baser kind
> By bud of nobler race. This is an art
> Which does mend Nature, change it rather, but
> The art itself is Nature.

Art itself is nature. It plays, as Spenser said not long before these words were written, 'second Nature's part', and while it is totally different from Nature in the ordinary sense, which includes the artist's personality, his outlook and his intentions, it is part of a natural process which we can occasionally observe and which would be the greatest paradox of all, were it not 'itself Nature'.

The first of the five 'paradoxes' which you list at the outset is the cleavage between the man and the book. 'The work has long passed for a mirror of honour and virtue; the author appears to have been little better than a criminal.' Let us leave aside for the moment all questions of fact. The evidence on which the notion of Malory's 'immorality' rests is very slight indeed. Considering the state of justice in fifteenth-century England, even a conviction would not have been sufficient to prove that he was guilty of any of the charges brought against him; and there was in fact no conviction, or at least we have no record of one. Your own assessment of Malory's probable misdeeds is as fair a hypothesis as any that can reasonably be advanced in the present state of our knowledge. But even if he were as 'immoral' a character as some of his other biographers want him to be, what difference would this make to our understanding of his work? What except the romantic myth of the work being an expression of the 'whole man' makes you think that there would be anything abnormal about a cleavage between the man and the book? I should have thought that it would be more contrary to the natural course of things if there were no such cleavage, for in that case the two 'natures' would be identical, whereas in fact they hardly ever are: no reader of your *Personal Heresy in Criticism* will ever take their identity for granted. Proust in his *Méthode de Sainte-Beuve* contrasts them as two distinct entities, totally unlike one another:

> Cette méthode, qui consiste à ne pas séparer l'homme et l'œuvre [. . .] méconnaît ce qu'une fréquentation un peu profonde avec nous-mêmes nous apprend: qu'un livre est le produit *d'un autre moi* que celui que nous manifestions dans nos habitudes [. . .] Ce *moi* profond qui a attendu pendant qu'on était avec les autres, on sent bien qu'il est *le seul réel*, celui pour lequel seul les artistes finissent par vivre, comme un dieu qu'ils quittent de moins en moins [. . .] Le *moi* de l'écrivain ne se montre que dans ses livres.

Proust is here speaking of authors about whose behaviour and character we can discover everything there is to be known; and his contention is that the more we concentrate on their *moi extérieur*, the less likely we are to understand their creative self, their *moi profond*. On this showing it seems singularly fortunate that our knowledge of Malory the man is not only limited but apparently inconsistent with the nature of his work: we are not even tempted to explain one through the other. It is, as you put it, 'a desperate expedient' to question Malory's identity simply because we cannot square the known facts of his life with the meaning and the message of his book; desperate to the extent of being perverse. Malory's biography has its uses: it is entertaining in itself, and it is an interesting sidelight on the social history of his time. But to feel 'disconcerted' about it as, for instance, E. K. Chambers did, is to misuse the results of biographical research, which are no more—and no less—puzzling in this case than such results normally are.

Your second and fourth 'paradoxes' are more difficult to dispose of, if indeed they can be disposed of at all. The problem they raise is a fundamental one. You find a curious contrast between Malory's efforts 'to eliminate the marvellous and introduce the humdrum' and the result of these efforts (Paradox II), and you suggest that there is an equally curious contrast between what seems to be a 'deeply religious' handling of the Grail story and a constant tendency to evade the religious issue (Paradox IV). What you say is not only true, but illuminating and very important. In Malory the feeling of the marvellous is not lessened, but intensified in spite of his 'practical realism'; and again, in his version of the Quest of the Holy Grail, much as he tries to cut down the religious exposition and even substitute the worldly for the divine, he produces a work which makes a more deeply religious impression on one's mind than the strictly orthodox original upon which it is based. How does this come about? I think you have supplied the answer. The work is not 'what any single individual either intended or foresaw'. 'Though every part of it was made by a man, the whole has rather grown than been made. Such things have a kind of existence that is almost midway between the works of art and those of nature.' I hope these words will long be remembered by all those who read Malory and induce others to read him. Perhaps you will allow me to illustrate them by a brief quotation:

> Lorde, I thanke The, for now I se that that hath be my desire many a day. Now, my Blessed Lorde, I wold nat lyve in this wrecched worlde no lenger, if hit myght please The, Lorde.

This is Galahad's last prayer, and perhaps one of the most profoundly religious moments ever recorded in any version of the Grail story. If you look at the corresponding place in Pauphilet's edition of the *Queste del Saint Graal*[1] you will find that every single word used by Malory is there, but that about three-quarters of the French text is missing in Malory. Among the omissions there are some important phrases and sentences which by the strict standards of the author of the French *Queste* the occasion required. And yet when you read the two passages together you realize that one has a power and a greatness totally absent from the other. Is this not, in miniature, the process you are thinking of? But why contrast in this instance 'art' and 'nature'? Why not say

[1] P. 278. I have quoted both passages in *Arthurian Literature in the Middle Ages* (Oxford, 1959) published since I wrote this letter (p. 548).

with Polixenes that this is 'an art that Nature makes'? The discrepancy between the intention and the result occurs daily in every branch of art, not because nature 'takes over' from the artist, but because the artist's genius takes control of the situation and modifies what we call his intention—his conscious self, his 'design'. It is again art 'playing second nature's part', acting much in the same way as nature is supposed to act, but *within* the artist's mind. Malory the man was certainly not a believer in the supernatural: the simple method of collation shows how consistently he cut it down in adapting his French books. And he was certainly not interested in the complexities of the Grail doctrine, as the same method amply demonstrates. But when we say this we describe the mind—or what happened in the mind—of Sir Thomas Malory when he was thinking about the supernatural and the Grail: we do *not* describe the process of his work, which is something very different and much more difficult to understand. The greater the author and the theme, the more room there is for this inner logic of the work, which alone, in the last analysis, determines the 'result'. It is the logic of the supernatural and the logic of the Grail theme that make the work into 'something which none of its successive builders intended or foresaw', but that logic only becomes active in the artist's hands; when it defeats his intentions and his beliefs the triumph is his: it is the triumph of his art over his conscious self, and each time it occurs he may well experience a 'more profound delight' in the result than the French authors had ever known.

Perhaps for the sake of clarity I ought to put it another way. If I understand your reasoning correctly, it is something like this: there was an excess of the supernatural in Malory's French originals; because he was out of sympathy with the supernatural he reduced the overall amount of it, and because 'two enchanters, two ghosts, two ferlies are always half as impressive as one' the reduction added to the impressiveness of the marvellous. But does this mean that anybody applying the same equation ($2 = \frac{1}{2}$) to the same material might achieve the same result? Surely not. And if you agree, that is to say, if you think as I do that the equation taken by itself is inoperative, would you not say that it became operative in Malory because of something that happened *in* Malory and did not happen elsewhere—something that for want of a better word we call his art? The equation is, of course, a paradox, and a splendid one, but not the process which makes the equation work. The essence of it is the co-existence of two 'natures', the conscious and the creative, one 'mending' the other—clearly something rare, but no more paradoxical or accidental than any art 'which adds to Nature'. This is not a criticism, but a development of your argument. Alone among critics you have perceived the significance of Malory's treatment of the supernatural and the religious, and the interpretation I suggest is simply a means of describing this treatment in more explicit terms while 'walking stumblingly' after you.

The two remaining sections—III and V—are no less illuminating and thought-provoking. You formulate your 'paradox V' as follows:

> Malory seemed to Saintsbury (and doubtless to many) the man who alone 'makes of this vast assemblage of stories one story and one book'. The evidence of the Winchester MS. convinces Professor Vinaver that he really wrote several works which were never intended to form a whole.

A thorny problem, and one which has engaged the attention of a considerable number of critics ever since I published my edition of the *Works*. But it seems to me that you have found the answer—if you can bear another paradox—by saying that you are 'bogged down in a preliminary doubt as to what precisely the question is'. Malory would have been 'bogged down' in very much the same doubt. It would be no use asking him, if he came back to life, 'how many books he thought he had written; he would think we meant the material volumes or "quairs". . . . If we talked to him about "artistic unity" he would not understand.' And you put the entire problem in a nutshell when you say: 'We should by the very form of our questions be presupposing concepts his mind was not furnished with.' But there are two issues we might consider: (*a*) how did Malory intend his romances to be presented to his readers? and (*b*) do these romances *in fact* make one romance? From the editor's point of view the first question is the only one that matters; the critic, on the other hand, is—or should be—interested primarily, if not exclusively, in the second, i.e. in the result, not in the intention. And either question can be answered without prejudice to the other.

What Malory *intended* could have been gathered long ago from his own words had they not been partly distorted in the process of transmission and partly misunderstood—or ignored. The Pierpont Morgan copy of Caxton's edition is the only existing record of what Malory wrote in his last colophon. In the other extant copy—the John Rylands—the last pages are missing. They have been replaced by Whittaker's facsimiles, which Sommer reproduced in his reprint, and everybody has since looked upon Sommer's text as a convenient and entirely reliable substitute for Caxton's. Unfortunately it is not at all reliable and the fault is not Sommer's, but Whittaker's. The Pierpont Morgan copy reads as follows:

> Here is the ende of the hoole book of kyng arthur and of his noble knyghtes of the rounde table that whan they were hole togyders there was euer an hondred and forty And here is the ende of the deth of arthur

The word *hoole* is the last word on the last page but one of the text; it is perfectly legible, but if one is a little careless, and especially if one is thinking of the next word (the first on the following page)—*book*—one can easily misread *hoole* as *booke*. This is precisely what Whittaker did. In Sommer we find, as a result, *here is the ende of the booke book*, which all later editors took for a dittography and reduced to *here is the end of the book*. Next came the critics who, looking at the passage, decided, quite naturally, that from Malory's point of view the 'book of King Arthur', &c., was the same as the 'Death of Arthur': that the words after the first *the ende of* were a description of the work of which the words after the second *the ende of* supplied the title. Hence, they concluded, Malory did give his romances one general title, and Caxton did not betray the author's intentions by saying in his own colophon: 'Thus endeth thys noble and Ioyous book entytled le morte Darthur.' There was clearly no harm in 'anglo-normanizing' *the death of*. Who can say, then, that Malory did not intend to write one book or that *Le Morte Darthur* is not its legitimate title?

I am not suggesting that without Whittaker's error critics would not have accepted Caxton's title and all that it involves, or even that the belief in Malory's 'unifying' design, shared by so many and denied by so few, rests to any appreciable extent on Malory's colophon; but I do think that now that we have at last got the correct reading of this colophon we ought to take some notice of it. Its implication seems to me crystal-clear. On the one hand there is 'the whole book', the entire collection, or series, of romances about King Arthur and his knights; and on the other, there is the *Death of Arthur*, the last work in the series, which presumably stands in the same relation to the whole as does each one of the romances—or 'works'—that occur earlier on. If we add to this the fact that, as the Winchester MS. shows, each romance has a separate title given to it in its colophon, that five out of the eight colophons end with the word *Amen* —the medieval equivalent of THE END—that four of these plus one other give the author's name (the equivalent of the signature with which not so long ago authors used to conclude their books), can there be much argument as to what Malory *intended* 'the whole book' to be? I am deliberately refraining for the moment from any discussion of its internal 'unity' or lack of 'unity': I am concerned purely and simply with what the text was meant to be; in other words I am arguing as an editor, not as a critic. And as an editor I feel that Malory has given us as clear an indication as any medieval author has ever done as to how his text should be presented to his readers. The only hesitation one might have concerns the words *the whole book of King Arthur and of his noble knights that when they were wholly together there was ever a hundred and forty*. Is this a title or a description of the series? My own feeling is—but I may be wrong—that both the qualifying adjective 'whole' and the subordinate clause after 'knights' tip the balance against the 'title' theory, and this is why I did not think I would be justified in replacing *Le Morte Darthur* (which, incidentally, *nobody* used as a title after Caxton until Haslewood revived it in 1816) by another title. I called my edition *The Works of Sir Thomas Malory*, which is clearly not a 'title'. You say, quite rightly, 'I do not for a moment believe that Malory had any intention either of writing a single "work" or of writing many "works" as we should understand the expression.' Of course not. But what author ever starts off with the idea of writing 'many works'? Can you honestly say that you ever did? And yet, if at some not distant date there appears a series of volumes entitled *The Works of C. S. Lewis* will you regard it as something contrary to your intentions as a writer?

I now come to the other and perhaps more important aspect of the problem: the 'critical' as distinct from the 'editorial'. I agree entirely with your concluding remarks: 'It is our imagination, not his (Malory's), that makes the work one or eight or fifty. We can read it either way. We can read it now one way, now another. We partly make what we read.' *We partly make what we read* describes a general phenomenon; what matters to us at the moment is the particular phenomenon: *We can read it now one way, now another*. We certainly can, but why? My explanation would be that the kind of 'unity' that people occasionally look for, and find, in Malory's romances is not the essential or the 'binding' kind. It is a kind without which any one of his romances could very well exist and be appreciated to the full. Remove from Malory's text all the occasional references to what is going to happen in a later work or to what has happened already in an earlier one, and nothing of importance will be lost. You are right in saying that some of these references are 'singularly fortunate', and it does not matter at this point in the argument whether they are of Malory's own making or whether they come straight from his sources: we are discussing the effect of the work, not its genesis. But by and large I can see only two 'areas' in which these references occur in a way that is at all significant: between the *Tale of King Arthur* and the *Quest of the Holy Grail* and between the *Quest* and the romance that comes immediately after it, *The Book of Sir Lancelot and Queen Guinevere*. The examples you quote are from the latter area; other critics have made a good deal of those which occur in the former.

I cannot help feeling that too much has been read into some of these examples. Does the sentence 'and ever Sir Launcelote wepte, as he had bene a chylde that had bene beatyn' in *The Healing of Sir Urry* really mean that 'as he failed in the Quest, so (for the same reason) he is failing now'? Lancelot has healed Sir Urry after everyone else has failed in the attempt. He and all the 'kings and knights' kneel down and give 'thankynges and lovynge unto God and unto Hys Blyssed Modir'. And tears—not, I think, of sorrow or contrition, but of joy and gratitude, flow down Lancelot's face. What can be more natural? And why think of the Quest at this point, and of Lancelot's failure in it, when there is not the slightest indication in the text that any such thoughts crossed his mind? I mention this example simply because so much has been made of it by the champions of 'unity' (E. K. Chambers was, I think, the first to suggest the interpretation which you have adopted). But there are, of course, others which cannot be dismissed, and which I have no intention of querying. Lancelot certainly refers to the Quest in speaking to Guinevere (*W* 1046.3–14), and Malory in describing the effects of the Dolorous Stroke clearly refers to the Grail theme (*W* 85.27–9). There are other reminders and anticipations of the same kind. But how much do they really mean to Malory's readers? Not to compilers of concordances, nor to Ph.D. candidates who laboriously dig them out and exhibit them as precious finds, but to people who read Malory as he was meant to be read, that is to say for pleasure, as a 'noble and joyous book'? I am sure you have guessed already the thought behind this question, but let me make it clearer still. In a work such as the Arthurian Cycle of romances commonly known as the 'Vulgate'—the great cycle containing the *Estoire del Graal*, the *Merlin*, the *Lancelot* proper, the *Queste del Saint Graal*, and the *Mort Artu*—references and cross-links of this kind not only occur more frequently, but have an entirely different function: without them the work would not make sense; it could be neither understood nor enjoyed (this, incidentally, is the reason why critics who have not taken the trouble to follow them up find the Vulgate unreadable). Hence there is, I think, some justification for calling such a composition 'one work'; none of it could be appreciated by a reader who did not carry the whole of it in his head. I have often wondered whether the changes in the form of the European novel are not determined, in the last analysis, by the variations in the quantity of things that one *can* carry in one's head: our modern novel does seem to correspond to our present capacity, while the thirteenth-century cyclic novel leaves us far behind, just as it left Malory and his readers far behind. Of course, it is always pleasant to be reminded in passing of something one remembers; but it is also pleasant to know that it does not really matter whether one remembers it or not, and this is what to my mind makes Malory's echoes from one work to another 'singularly fortunate'. It would be disastrous if we made the entire edifice of his romances rest upon them: *Le Morte Darthur* would immediately collapse. If we don't want this to happen we must not let our imagination 'make the work one'; but on the other hand, it would be a pity if we lost altogether the feeling which you describe so well in your Preface to extracts from Spenser in *Major British Writers*, the feeling that 'adventures of this sort are going on all round us, that in this vast forest (we are nearly always in a forest) this is the sort of thing that goes on all the time, that it was going on before we arrived and will continue after we have left'.

Here, then, the achievement, the final result is not in any way contrary to the intention: we read Malory more or less as he thought one ought to read him, and enjoy the arrangement and the somewhat capricious sequence of romances as he intended it to be enjoyed. The difficulty upon which so much thought and effort have been expended in recent years does not arise (and this is indeed a paradox) until we 'presuppose concepts Malory's mind was not furnished with' either at the reflective or at the creative level.

There is much the same relationship between intention and achievement in his narrative technique (Paradox III). You agree that he made a valiant effort to 'straighten out' the unbelievably complex pattern of interwoven narratives which he found in his French books. If he had not done this very few people in post-medieval England would have bothered to read him, just as in post-medieval France very few people have bothered to read in the original the great Arthurian Cycle of the thirteenth century. Of course, he did not carry the process of straightening-out to the end; and of course it is true that such 'interweavings' as he left in the text often add to our enjoyment of it. But it is entirely a question of degree: he carried his modifications far enough to make the work 'pleasant to read in' by modern standards. Here again the reader's reaction is conditioned partly by the author's efforts and partly by what he allowed to survive from the earlier state of his stories. With all its component elements and techniques the work has grown, as you say, 'into something strange and admirable', something which none of its successive builders can claim to have foreseen exactly as it is. This great cathedral 'stands solidly before us' and imposes upon us a structure of its own. Nothing else survives. Many writers had worked on the French Arthurian prose romances between the thirteenth and the fifteenth centuries; there had been adaptations of it in Spain and in Germany. All this is now dead and buried, and Malory alone stands as a rock defying all changes of taste and style and morals; not as a grand paradox of nature, but as a lasting work of art. Is it not, then, right that we should be thinking of the work in terms of what *he* did when he called it back to life? To create does not necessarily mean to invent or even to build; it may mean to leave out or to undo what others have done; it may even be something less tangible, which somehow transforms what had no existence into something that has. And our task as interpreters is really much more modest than people think. We can neither define nor explain. But we can point in the direction where we feel the path of genius lies and hope that in this way we may bring ourselves and others a little closer to its understanding. This is what you have done. Hence my gratitude.

Yours,

EUGÈNE VINAVER.

4

'the hoole book'

D. S. BREWER

WHEN *The Works of Sir Thomas Malory* appeared, the title gave us both a sense of relief and an unpleasant shock. It was a relief to find how the concept of eight separate romances seemed to clarify what had before seemed muddled and inconsistent. It seemed to explain the apparent resurrections of once slaughtered knights, and the introduction of knights full-grown whose birth and upbringing are only recounted later. Even more, the nature of Malory's literary achievement, of the way he broke down the interwoven cyclic romances that were his sources, became clearer and more enjoyable. But it was also disagreeable to find that what we had been brought up on as one book, however muddled, was now supposed to be eight distinct books. Part of this response may have been no more than the natural reaction to the disturbance of set ideas. Nevertheless, even now, when we are used to the idea of there being eight entirely separate romances, when all the advantages of the theory have been considered, a careful examination of Malory's work makes one doubt it. Illuminated and indeed convinced as one is bound to be by Professor Vinaver's brilliant display of Malory's treatment of his sources, no one, surely, 'uncorrupted with literary prejudices after all the refinements of subtilty and the dogmatism of learning' can avoid an impression of *The Works* as one book —'the hoole book' as Caxton called it. It is not quite that one disagrees with the theory of the limited separateness of the tales, but that one is bound to reject what seem to be the implications of Professor Vinaver's thesis—that Malory's romances are as separate as the various novels of a modern author; that the romances may be taken in any or no particular order; and that they have no cumulative effect.

Our difficulty in discussing the form of the *Morte Darthur* is partly due to the lack of satisfactory descriptive and critical terms for the kind of literary experience that Malory gives us. It is natural for those who are dissatisfied with the idea of completely separate romances to assert some kind of unity for Malory's work. But obviously unity here cannot mean structural unity of a kind we expect from a modern novel, or that we find in an ancient epic; and the term unity (which I have used in the past) is probably misleading and should be abandoned. If we assert the connectedness of the constituent works we shall be on safer ground, but there are not specific connexions everywhere, and the term does not include those impressions of unity of atmosphere and of underlying concepts which Professor Vinaver himself has never denied, and which are an important part of the general literary effect. Perhaps the best term, of a useful elasticity, is *cohesion*.[1] The cohesion of Malory's *Works* is greater than that of the separate works of a modern novelist, though it is different from that Coleridgean concept of 'organic unity' with which we now approach a work of art.

The emphasis must be on 'the work of art'. In the last resort, when all has been learnt that can be known of authorship and source, Malory's work must be judged, like any other, in and for itself alone. It is the more important to emphasize this in Malory's case because, as Professor Vinaver has shown us, Malory had a peculiar relation to his sources. He has rehandled them, to be sure, in accordance with his own strong feeling for form and moral content, but he is also completely at their mercy. Unless they move him, he cannot move. The essence of the matter was put by a reviewer of Vinaver's edition in *The Times Literary Supplement* (7 June 1947): 'we are not reading the work of an independent artist. . . . Whatever he does, Malory's personal contribution to the total effect cannot be very great, though it may be very good.' When we look at Malory's work—or works—we are not looking at the work of one man, but perhaps of a dozen, far separated in time and space, occupation

[1] Professor Vinaver has himself suggested the use of this term to me. I am grateful to him for this and for several other suggestions generously made to me on the subject of this essay.

and outlook. Each writer built on what had been made before. The work of art is cumulative and transcends any one, or any group, of its makers. Malory's very dependence on his sources makes us insist, paradoxically, that in terms of art neither the sources nor Malory himself are of the least importance. Malory's personal contribution is less than the book as a whole, and the book may create effects of which Malory is little more than the scribe.

Here is perhaps the root of the differences, which, after all, are rather of emphasis and nomenclature than of principle, between Professor Vinaver and those who are reluctant to accept the complete divisions proposed in his great edition of 1947 and further emphasized in his edition of *The Death of King Arthur*. In his major edition Professor Vinaver was chiefly concerned to show the nature and as it were the machinery of Malory's personal contribution. That he has brilliantly succeeded, and in so doing has made an important contribution to our understanding of Malory's work, and of an important phase in literary history, is beyond dispute. But it may also be argued that in his perfectly proper and highly illuminating emphasis on Malory's personal contribution, and perhaps because of his own vast knowledge of the whole Arthurian *corpus*, he has taken for granted what needs equal emphasis in an aesthetic judgement: that is, the inherent tendencies to cohesion of that *corpus*, and Malory's reflection of that tendency to cohesion, even while he simplified its complexities. His simplification, indeed inevitably made the cohesion more evident.

Yet I do not wish to underestimate Malory's personal contribution even to the sense of cohesion in the whole Arthurian *corpus*. At the very least he brought out what was only suggested, and the completed work shows that his whole attitude to the material differed from his predecessors'. Professor Vinaver's consciousness of Malory's dependence on, yet divergence from, his sources sometimes leads him to measure Malory against the French and find him wanting, where to the less learned reader it seems merely that Malory is attempting and achieving something different. A minor example of this is Malory's detail of the twenty thousand pounds it cost the Queen to find Lancelot (*W* 831), which

Professor Vinaver once deplored and Professor Lewis defended. Granted the different premises, each critic is right. But if we judge Malory's work by the standards of its source, rather than by its effectiveness within its own context, we may miss, or misinterpret, the special quality of the work of art itself.

Thus for two opposite reasons, Malory's dependence on his sources, and Malory's differences from his sources, we must make a clear distinction between Malory's personal contribution and the actual book he left. Sometimes the effect of the book is due primarily to Malory's source, and sometimes it is due primarily to Malory's own personal contribution. Fascinating and important as it is to distinguish, guided by Professor Vinaver, between what is derived and what is personal,[1] such a distinction cannot affect our final judgement on the total work of art, which must be judged in its own right, as a whole, obeying its own laws, holding and shaping the reader's imagination by its own power. (I do not deny the value of anything that will help us to a clearer understanding of the work of art, especially in places where it is obscure or to some extent unsuccessful; a knowledge of the sources is particularly relevant to understanding much of Malory, and the knowledge that Professor Vinaver has put at our disposal enormously increases our understanding and enjoyment of Malory's aims and achievements.)

When, therefore, we disregard the peculiar mixture of source and personal contribution in Malory's book, and look 'at the thing in itself, as it really is', we shall be more than ever impressed by a sense of its cohesion. How far that impression is due to Malory's sources does not for the moment matter. It would not even matter if Malory's personal contribution had only been to attempt to break down that sense of cohesion; it is still there. And in fact the case is not so desperate. It is possible to show, thanks to Professor Vinaver's own edition, that there are bonds still left between the various tales, and that Malory also made a deliberate attempt to link the beginnings and ends of his tales together. It is also possible to show that the tales could

[1] The distinction is obviously artificial; in fact the two may merge indistinguishably. Nevertheless, the two elements exist separately.

not have been put together in any order other than the present one; that the succession of romances has a cumulative effect; and that there is a kind of shapeliness in the whole book, even though the shape is one that is difficult to describe.

We must first emphasize what is indeed indisputable, the unity of tone and atmosphere, the continual moral concern of a special kind. All the tales are concerned with the romance of knight-errantry, of strange adventures in which the wrongs of the oppressed are to be righted, and in which the High Order of Knighthood is justified and glorified. There is certainly a development in Malory's concept of true morality, and certainly the earlier books are fiercer, more primitive; but the same conception of the moral quality of knightliness, most movingly expressed in Ector's lament for Lancelot, underlies them all.

Then all the stories are concerned with the same kind of people, and all these people are associated with the same central group, the court of Arthur. Indeed, one of Malory's great achievements is his portrayal of this passionate, limited and aristocratic society, with its own standards of success and failure.

Next, within this society some half-dozen characters are dominant in most of the tales and continually recur. Of these Arthur and Lancelot are the most important. Now it is very noticeable that the tales, in the order that we have them, observe the proper sequence of events in the lives of Lancelot and Arthur. There is a biographical continuity observed throughout the tales which effectively links them together. This is worth exploring. Its existence reduces to minor proportions certain apparent inconsistencies in the treatment of minor characters. There are no inconsistencies (though perhaps some lack of realism) in the presentation, in due order, throughout all the tales, of the lives of the chief characters.

The passage of time, and the development of character and event are particularly strongly felt in the first two and last three tales. The first two tales show us the birth of Arthur, his first flowering as a knight, and his triumph as a great king over many lands—though with this essential theme there are, in Spenserian terms, 'other adventures intermedled'. The second tale, of Arthur's war against Rome, is especially interesting because in it the young Lancelot appears for the first time. He is rapidly brought forth as a hero subsidiary to Arthur alone; and Professor Vinaver shows that Malory invents almost everything that is said about Lancelot in this tale, while diminishing the roles that other knights have in his source. At the end of the second tale Arthur is triumphantly established as the greatest English king, ruling from Ireland to Rome, surrounded by his knights of the Round Table, devoted to the High Order of Knighthood. It seems to a reader natural and logical enough that the third tale should go on to establish in his own right the prowess of Malory's second hero, Sir Lancelot. Once Lancelot is established, the next tales reinforce the sense of continuity by going on to give the histories and to reveal the glorious deeds of other knights of the Round Table. These are the short tale of Sir Gareth and the inordinately long one of Sir Tristram. The reason why Malory leaves out the tragic end of the French tale of Sir Tristram, and leaves Sir Tristram in cheerful domesticity, is surely because these central tales of Lancelot, Gareth, Tristram, and a number of minor characters, are all devoted to the glory and success of the knights of the Round table. Arthur and Lancelot, once they have been established, recede somewhat into the background. But Arthur is the point of departure and return for all the knights, and their glory is his; while Sir Lancelot, even where he is not a central figure, is frequently mentioned as the type of ideal knight. The praise of Sir Tristram is that his fame at one time began to overshadow Sir Lancelot's, and there could be no higher praise. In these fourth and fifth books, therefore, if Arthur and Lancelot are less active it is not because they have been supplanted.

In all the French books, and in the English *Morte Arthure* which is the principal source of Malory's second tale, the story of the Roman campaign and triumph is followed forthwith by the story of Arthur's downfall. Malory places the story of Lancelot's adventures immediately after Arthur's return from Rome. Professor Vinaver argues from this that

Malory was ignorant of the position of the '*Lancelot* proper' in the Arthurian cycle (*W* 1398). But Malory knew, if only from the English source of his second tale, that the death of Arthur followed the Roman campaign, and he probably knew this from French tales as well. The change he introduced was probably deliberate. He postponed the tragic end and turned his second tale into a tale of triumph, possibly in tribute, as Professor Vinaver suggests, to Henry V, but also in tribute to Arthur, and to all that Arthur stands for in his imagination. The triumphant second tale establishes the chief hierophant of the Order of Knighthood. Arthur has to be established in his own greatness before we feel the greatness of his court, his knights, and the ideals they express. On the other hand the crowning of Arthur is the climax of his personal triumph. Further adventures of his own could not effectively add to it. His glory is extended in the next three tales by the glorious deeds of his knights. These anglicized paladins, with their noble achievements, by acknowledging him as their lord add their renown to his. Certainly, Malory was not interested in subtle analysis of courtly feeling, but it is fruitless to blame him for this. We must take what we can get. What we are offered is essentially the story of the Golden Age of English history, and how it came to its tragic end. So it is fitting that the time of Arthur's triumph should be separated from the time of disaster. It makes Arthur's fame in later ages more comprehensible, it allows us to dwell somewhat on the English glory of the Round Table and of the Order of Knighthood. And as a literary result, it makes the final tragedy more moving by allowing to flourish somewhat the flower which is to be so cruelly lopped; for the final tragedy is not only one of persons but of 'the flower of chivalry of the world'; of a whole noble way of life.

After the second book there are no precise notations of age, but it is nevertheless true that we have been introduced to the chief actors in their youth, and that we follow them through the glory of their maturity to their sad decline and exemplary deaths. Within this general biographical chronology, which is never violated, inconsistencies in the treatment of some minor characters are unimportant. Such as they are (and they have been over-emphasized) they tend to occur in the middle books, where the sense of the passage of time, though not neglected by Malory, is less important. Thus, taking the events in the lives of Arthur and Lancelot as our main guide, we can see a clearly perceptible progression throughout the first two books, which corresponds to the rise in Fortune's wheel; a less perceptible movement in the next three books, when Arthur's glory is at its height; and a further progressive movement in the last three books, gathering momentum especially in the last two, whose downward movement is the wheel's adverse turn. Whether or not Malory consciously intended this form is perhaps disputable. If he did not, he would not be the first or last author to have built better than he knew. In any event, Malory's conscious intentions are undiscoverable and unimportant, except in so far as they reveal themselves in the book. The test of the form I have suggested is whether it corresponds to the details of the book; whether it makes sense in itself; and whether equal sense could be made of a different arrangement of the books.

The form makes sense in itself because it describes a general chronological progression just like those in life, and also comprehensible to medieval views of life. Growth, flowering, and decay; rise, supremacy, and fall not only completely accord with normal experience, but can easily be imaged in such medieval terms as Fortune's wheel. If we disorder the tales, this general pattern which holds them together is lost. And to insist on the completely separate nature of the *Works* is inevitably to insist that there is no literary value in reading them in any specific order; to insist that there will be no loss if we read of Arthur's death, before we read of his triumph or birth. How can we insist on such a crippling procedure, once we have realized the chronological order of the tales in their present sequence?

In looking more closely at the details of arrangement we should bear in mind that for Malory the material he was arranging was historical material. For various reasons medieval writers make a different distinction from ours between *fabula* and *historia*; or rather, the two kinds intermingled for them in a way that is strange to us.

Chaucer's treatment of the story of Troilus and Criseyde is perhaps the most obvious example, but there are many others.[1] Furthermore, it is well known that from the late twelfth to the early seventeenth centuries practically all Englishmen thought that Arthur was a genuinely historical figure; and it is clear both from the general situation and from his own remarks (e.g. *W* 1229) that Malory shared this view. Caxton in his Preface to the *Morte Darthur* 'coude not wel denye but that there was suche a noble kyng named Arthur'. He refers to Malory's work as 'a joyous history', even if 'to gyve fayth and byleve that al is trewe that is conteyned herein, ye be at your liberté'. Malory is not writing a work—or, not to beg the question, even works—of 'pure' fiction; nor is he writing an historical novel. Yet he is not writing chronicle-history either. His relation to the historical 'truth' may be compared to Shakespeare's. Shakespeare's handling of history is that of an artist: he feels free to embroider; but he does not go against the essential historical truth as it is known to him. Shakespeare, also, knew three types of history. First, relatively recent English history; second, Roman history (each of these being fairly realistically chronicled in their differing degrees); and third, legendary history, mostly English, though it included the story of Hamlet as well as that of Lear and Cymbeline. There is no reason to think that the third type seemed any less genuinely historical to the Elizabethans than the first two, but it was obviously much less authoritatively recorded, with less realistic detail, and consequently gave far greater freedom of interpretation and invention. We are greatly in Professor Vinaver's debt for his valuable account of the way in which medieval writers varied the interpretation of a given story; but it does not seem that the use of interpretation and invention destroyed the feeling of history, of basic historical fact, for Malory any more than for the authors of *Troilus and Criseyde*, *Paradise Lost*—or the gospel of St John. For all his recasting, the effect of Malory's treatment of his subject was if anything to increase its historical nature. This is

[1] Cf. my *Chaucer*, 3rd edition, 1961, pp. 95, 127, 148, 158, for examples from Chaucer.

partly the result of a rather factual turn of imagination, as seen, for example, in the famous 'twenty thousand pounds'. It is also the result of his chronological treatment, through the series of tales in their order as we have them, of the birth, life, acts, and death of the greatest English king, who created, with his knights, the High Order of Knighthood. By and through the life and death of Arthur, Malory half created from the interwoven threads of his sources something quite different from what he found—a pattern of tragedy, and a tragedy in history.

It is this 'historical' basis that does much to explain our sense of the cohesion of Malory's separate tales. It would be strange, however, if this cohesion rested only on general impressions, and the general course of the narrative. It does not. There is plenty of evidence in the actual conduct of the individual stories, in the actual words that Malory uses, which confirms our feeling, and which is indeed largely the basis of our feeling, that with whatever local failure to master the material, Malory is dealing with one tract of time, one general course of events, throughout the whole series of tales. This evidence is found in the numerous references back and forth which establish continuity and connexions throughout the various books; and in the deliberate links invented by Malory, which form bridges between the main tales, and which further confirm the need to read them in the order in which they have come down to us.

To take some of the references forward and back. In the first tale, at the end of its first section, there is a reference forward to Mordred coming to court 'as hit rehersith aftirward and towarde the ende of the MORTE ARTHURE' (*W* 56). This comment is apparently not in the French original. It may refer either to the French *Mort Artu* or to Malory's own later version. If to the latter, Professor Vinaver suggests that the comment is a scribal insertion not due to Malory himself. But the comment appears in both Caxton's text and the Winchester MS., and there is no evidence that it is merely scribal. It is at least as likely to be Malory's as not. Even if Malory's, it may be due to a phrase in the actual book he was copying. But it does not matter; the effect of a phrase like this in Malory's work as we have it, whether or not in eight parts, is to bind the parts together. The likely reason for the remark, if it is indeed Malory's, is surely that he was thinking forward not particularly to his own translation, if he projected it, but to the 'future' event which was part of the whole historical Arthurian sequence, whose cohesion underlies his work. There are a number of other references to 'future' events in this first tale (for example, on pages 91, 92, 97, 126, 179–80). Some of these are unquestionably due to 'the French book'. But as I have emphasized, it is immaterial for the present purpose whether such remarks are original or due to the source, since we are dealing with a work of multiple authorship, not Malory's alone. Whether or not invented or even intended by Malory, the binding effect is there. Thus, granting all that Professor Vinaver has shown us of Malory's reducing, dissolving, simplifying power, Malory has not cut the bonds completely. He has at least left in, or put in, those references forward of which I have given examples. In at least one case he has made the reference more explicit than it was in the French, as Professor Vinaver shows us:

> Marlyon warned the kyng covertly that Gwenyvere was nat holsom for hym to take to wyff. For he warned hym that Launcelot scholde love hir, and sche hym agayne (*W* 97).

The French original of this is a very obscure hint, which Malory makes perfectly plain—somewhat to the disadvantage, indeed, of Arthur's character. Malory's clarification is not the kind of remark that reveals a modern sense of organic unity in the structure of the 'whole book', but it helps to establish, like the other references forward, a sense that we are dealing with a specific tract of experience, a history linked in cause and effect. That these references come so early in the whole historical sequence surely indicates that for Malory the various stories were bound together.

It does not matter that some of the references forward are inaccurate (e.g. that on pp. 179–80): no one can be surprised if an author whose scope is so vast changes the details of his plans. These references are inaccurate inasmuch as they do not agree with the later version produced by Malory himself, because they are translated from the source Malory was following at that moment, the *Suite du Merlin*, and they refer to the Quest of the Grail. From these inaccuracies Professor Vinaver argues Malory's ignorance, when writing this first tale, of the true story of the Grail, or at least of the version he was himself to translate, perhaps years later. Even if Professor Vinaver is right, we need not be driven to denying Malory's consciousness of the total Arthurian context. He cannot have been totally ignorant of the Grail story and its effect on the story of Arthur. At the very least these references he translates would have told him a good deal in outline. And would so devoted a reader of Arthurian tales have remained in ignorance of so well known a story even if, as is not surprising, he was hazy about the details?

Just as there are references forward in the first tale there are references back in the later tales. Some of the most notable are in *The Tale of the Sankgreal* itself, where, for example, Malory, apparently unprompted by his source, deliberately refers back to the story of Balin, which is part of the first tale (*W* 856ff., especially 862–3). There are similar backward glances in the final *Tale of the Death of King Arthur* (e.g. p. 1198, referring to pp. 265–6). Again, these are more like an historian's references to earlier significant incidents and causes, than an artist's attempt to build up an organic whole. But these connexions have an artistic effect; they give a sense of continuity and also, as it were, of depth. They show the effects of causes remote but not detached. They give that sense of context in human affairs which great literature usually suggests.

Besides these references forward and back there are also specific links between several of the tales which prove that Malory did not think of them as being entirely separate, and which show that he must have intended them to be read in the order in which they have come down to us. Thus, the concluding paragraph, or *explicit*, of the first tale runs:

> And this book endyth whereas sir Launcelot and sir Trystrams com to courte. Who that woll make ony more lette hym seke other bookis of kynge Arthure or of sir Launcelot or sir Trystrams: for this was drawyn by a knyght presoner, sir Thomas Malleoré, that God sende hym good recover. Amen EXPLICIT (*W* 180).

If it is perhaps too much to say quite so definitely as does Professor Vinaver that Malory here 'disclaims any intention of writing another Arthurian romance' (*W* xxx), it certainly looks as though he did not expect the opportunity to write more very soon, even though he new what his sources would be. But before theorizing about this *explicit* one should look at the very first paragraph of the next tale, *Arthur and Lucius*, to compare its very phrasing:

> Hyt befelle whan kyng Arthur had wedded quene Gwenyvere and fulfylled the Rounde Table, and so aftir his mervelous knyghtis and he had venquyshed the moste party of his enemyes, than *sone aftir com sir Launcelot de Lake unto the courte, and sir Trystrams come that tyme also.* . . . (*W* 185: italics mine.)

This introductory paragraph clearly gathers up what has preceded and so establishes a chronological development; and what is especially notable is that the phrase about Lancelot and Tristram (which has no counterpart in the French) directly refers to the preceding *explicit*. Malory has created a deliberate link.

It is odd that this deliberate link to some extent seems to contradict the implication in the preceding *explicit* that the author cannot write any more. But Malory clearly worked with the French book in front of him, translating much of the time sentence by sentence, and if we imagine his imprisonment keeping him from the books he needed to continue his work (though he knew, at least roughly, what books they were), then we may have a possible solution to the puzzle. When he was released he was able to find the books he needed for continuation—though, ironically, it may have been a further spell of imprisonment which inflicted on him the necessary leisure. In any event, it is most unusual for a medieval writer to indicate further sources for the continuation—and we may emphasize 'continuation'—of his story. That Malory did so suggests that he had some sort of plan for the rest of his work, though it may well have been vague.[1]

There is also a link between the second and third tales.

[1] This is suggested by Professor Lumiansky, 'The Question of Unity in Malory's *Morte Darthur*', *Tulane Studies in English*, V (1955), p. 33.

The *explicit* of the second tale says that here is an end of this tale,

> And here folowyth afftyr many noble talys of sir Launcelot de Lake. (*W* 247)

And so, of course, they do, in the third tale, which takes up the story immediately at the correct point of time: soon after King Arthur's return from Rome, it begins, Sir Lancelot in especial increased marvellously in worship and honour. Therefore, says Malory,

> he is the fyrste knyght that the Frey[n]sh booke makyth me[n]cion of aftir kynge Arthure com frome Rome (*W* 253).

Malory loses no time bringing Lancelot to the fore, telling of the love between him and Guinevere, and mentioning how he saved her from the stake (which happens in both the seventh and eighth tales). It is not clear how far these introductory comments are Malory's own, since no very close source has yet been discovered. Judging from Malory's usual method they are very likely to be entirely his own; but it does not matter. Whether original or not these comments still place the tale in its wider context of the Arthurian story as a whole; and in doing so they establish the present tale as part of that whole. Of course, this kind of connexion is tenuous in certain respects. Professor Vinaver is perfectly right to insist on a high degree of autonomy in some of the tales. But the separation is not, could not be, complete.

Between the tale of *Sir Launcelot* and the next of *Sir Gareth* there is no specific link. There is, however, a vague indication of time: it begins:

> In Arthurs dayes, when he held the Rounde Table moste plenoure. . . . (*W* 293.)

The suggestion here is of the height of the success of the Round Table as an institution. Although there is no specific link with the preceding tale of *Sir Launcelot*, nor any link with the following tale of *Sir Tristram*, the tale of *Sir Gareth* could not come anywhere else than here. The first three tales have already been shown linked together by chronology and by specific references at the beginnings and ends. As will be shown, the fifth tale of *Sir Tristram* leads directly into the sixth, the *Sankgreal*, and that into the seventh and eighth tales. Even if the 'separate' tales had circulated in separate manuscripts, (for which, significantly, there is not a scrap of evidence) it would have been impossible in collecting them into one book to place the apparently unattached *Sir Gareth* anywhere but in the fourth place. This alone shows the existence of a wider scheme into which the tales must fit. They are related; not independent.

The fifth tale is that of *Sir Tristram*, and one of the objections to considering the tales as a connected series is that Sir Tristram appears as a full-grown man in the previous tale of *Sir Gareth* (and is indeed mentioned even earlier), while his birth and upbringing are not described until this fifth tale. Malory, indeed, is not much interested in giving mere chronology. The beginning of *Sir Tristram*, like the beginning of the preceding tale of *Sir Gareth*, is set in that long, vague period when Arthur was established as the great king of 'all the lordshyppis unto Roome' (*W* 371), and when Lancelot was 'named for the mervaylyste knyght of the worlde' (*W* 377). This is enough to put the tale in its context of the whole Arthurian story. Tristram's birth and arrival at manhood take place within this general period of the flourishing of the Round Table. This is unrealistic, of course, but no one can claim that romance is bound by the chains of realism. Professor Lumiansky has suggested that we should regard the account of Tristram's birth and so forth as 'retrospective narrative'.[1] Attractive as this theory is, there seems no evidence for it in the text. It is more likely that Malory regarded the bulky tale of *Sir Tristram* as being in some sense parallel to that of *Sir Gareth*. Or his technique, never very self-aware, was simply not up to the problem he had perhaps unwittingly set himself. He went steadily on, at the beginning of *Sir Tristram*, in a continuous narrative, content to let the wider time-scheme look after itself, since he was here concerned with neither Arthur's rise nor his fall, where chronology was more important.

The Book of Sir Tristram, which is rather more than a third

[1] Op. cit.

of the whole book, and comes right in the middle, is by general consent the least satisfactory of Malory's tales. If I were contending that there was a modern organic unity of design in Malory's work, the *Tristram* would in itself be enough to refute me. But my contention is more modest; less of a denial of Professor Vinaver's thesis than a modification or complement of it: the tales are structurally connected, and fit into a particular order. Thus, even the *Tristram*, such a stumbling block to attempts to define the general form of the whole book, is connected with the following tale of the Sankgreal, and by virtue of that connexion could occupy no other place in the chain than where it is found.

Towards the end of the *Tristram* comes the story of Lancelot and Elaine. If this story is judged in the context of the *Tristram* alone it is quite irrelevant, Sir Tristram being hardly mentioned. It begins with a hermit prophesying about the Siege Perilous and the winning of the Holy Grail, and then tells how Galahad, the future Grail-hero, was begotten on Elaine by Sir Lancelot, how Guinevere's jealousy sent Lancelot mad, and how he eventually recovered. The Grail itself also appears. All this is quite pointless if the *Tristram* exists for itself alone. The story of Lancelot and Elaine is there to enable us to understand the story of the Grail, which follows almost immediately. There is here a clear structural connexion. It is not Malory's invention; he is following his source. But that does not in any way weaken the effect of the connexion. Moreover, Professor Vinaver points out several interpolations by Malory which emphasize the relationship of the episode to the whole Arthurian Cycle (*W* 793, 794, 796, 832; cf. notes on pp. 1512 and 1518). Surely, had Malory wished completely to separate his tales he would have avoided such interpolations and would have transposed the story of Lancelot and Elaine to the beginning of the Grail Quest where, as simple narrative, it belongs?

Of course, Malory did no such thing. After telling how Galahad was begotten, he returned (following his source) to the tale of Tristram in a brief *Conclusion*. The interweaving is emphasized by La Belle Isode immediately telling Tristram about Lancelot's madness 'and how he was holpyn by the holy vessell of the Sankgreall'. Then she refers to the great feast to be held at Pentecost next following (which is where the story of the Quest of the Grail will begin), thus making clear the time-sequence where it is important. The end of the *Conclusion* tells how Tristram and Palomides set off for Arthur's court to attend the great feast,

> And that same feste in cam sir Galahad that was son unto sir Launcelot du Lake, and sate in the Syge Perelous. And so therewythall they departed and dysceyvirde, all the knyghtys of the Rounde Table.
>
> And than sir Trystram returned unto Joyus Garde, and sir Palomydes folowed aftir the Questynge Beste (*W* 845).

This neatly rounds off the tale of Tristram in Malory's accustomed manner, for the tragedy of Tristram was nothing to his purpose: yet even this passage acts as a bridge between the concluding tale and the next. The mention of Galahad and the Siege Perilous throws the interest forward, while it could only have meaning from the previous account of the begetting of Galahad. Granted the autonomy of the *Tristram*, we are yet left with the feeling that however long it may be, it is also a part of a yet longer, more complex story, that of Arthur's Round Table. We have come to a pause, not a full-stop.

The *explicit* which closes the tale, makes the same effect:

> Here endyth the secunde boke off syrr Trystram de Lyones, whyche drawyn was oute of Freynshe by sir Thomas Malleorré, knyght, as Jesu be hys helpe. Amen.
>
> But here ys no rehersall of the thirde booke.
>
> But here folowyth the noble tale off the Sankegreall, whyche called ys the holy vessell and the sygnyfycacion of blyssed bloode offe oure Lorde Jesu Cryste, whyche was brought into thys londe by Joseph off Aramathye . . . &c. (*W* 845).

The *explicit* has some of the oddity which is often found in Malory's prose when he is not dealing with narrative or dialogue. But the absence of the third book is not so odd as it seems, for the third book was itself a version of the Grail story. Malory abandoned it in favour of another version, essentially the same, but less prolix, and less concerned with Tristram. The *explicit*, however, clearly makes another bridge, and *The Tale of the Sankgreal* naturally takes up the narrative at the same feast of Pentecost already mentioned. The continuity is complete.

The Tale of the Sankgreal, sometimes incoherent, occasionally very moving, has many difficulties and puzzles, and it is not always easy to know how to take it. One thing is clear. As Professor Vinaver has shown, it is, unlike its source, essentially an Arthurian tale. It is not anti-chivalric, and Lancelot is the most interesting character (*W* 1522–3). Malory does not agree with his source that the chivalric ideal is anti-Christian. For Malory—and we shall never understand him if we do not undertand this—there is no essential incompatibility between the values of Christianity and those of the High Order of Knighthood, of ideal Arthurian chivalry. (Of course he realized that many knights, even Lancelot, fell below this ideal; and he himself seems to a modern reader to be sometimes lacking in moral scruple and insight; for example in the early parts of the *Tristram*.) In the Grail story, therefore, success is largely thought of in terms of the possible success of secular Christian knighthood, and failure again is seen in terms of failure to maintain normal Christian morality. Success and failure are summed up in the achievements of Lancelot. In so far as he succeeds it is because he is brave and good and repents of his sins. His failure is the result mainly of his adultery and consequent disloyalty to Arthur, which blemish his knighthood and eventually bring about the destruction of the king, the Round Table, and all it stood for. In a sense, perhaps, the story of the Grail is debased to an illustration of the quality, both good and bad, of Lancelot, though this would be to take an extreme view, and there is more than that in the tale. But it is certain that Malory rejects, or is not interested in, or does not understand, the transcendent quality of the Grail legend, and of its underlying theology, for he denies their lesson. He has the characteristic English tendency to turn other-worldly and ascetic religion into this-worldly morality. The story of the Grail enabled Malory to work out and emphasize the moral standards which underlie the tragedy towards which the whole Arthurian story moves. This tragedy is related in the two tales which follow *The*

Tale of the Sankgreal, and which are as closely linked between themselves, as the last but one is to the *Sankgreal.* Once again the continuity and connection is made clear by Malory in his words in the first paragraphs of *The Book of Sir Launcelot and Queen Guinivere*, which immediately follows on the *Sankgreal*:

So aftir the queste of the Sankgreall was fulfylled and all kynghtes that were leffte on lyve were com home agayne unto the Table Rounde—as the BOOKE OF THE SANKGREALL makith mencion—than was there grete joy in the courte. . . .

Than, as the booke seyth, sir Launcelot began to resorte unto quene Gwenivere agayne and forgate the promyse and the perfeccion that he made in the queste: for, as the booke seyth, *had nat sir Launcelot bene in his prevy thoughtes and in hys myndis so sette inwardly to the quene as he was in semynge outewarde to God, there had no knyght passed hym in the queste of the Sankgreall. But ever his thoughtis prevyly were on the quene. . . .*

So hit befelle that sir Launcelot had many resortis of ladyes and damesels which dayly resorted unto hym [that besoughte hym] to be their champion. In all such maters of ryght *sir Launcelot applyed hym dayly to do for the plesure of oure Lorde Jesu Cryst*, and ever as much as he myght he withdrew hym fro the company of quene Gwenyvere for to eschew the sclawndir and noyse. (*W* 1045: italics mine.)

There could be no clearer example than this of the sense of continuity between the tales, of their connectedness. And this passage also shows clearly the mixture of good and bad which Malory sees in Lancelot, brought out by his partial success, his partial failure, in the quest of the Grail. It may well be that Malory's treatment of the Grail legend is inferior in subtlety and intellectual power to that of his source, but the important thing is that Malory's treatment is different, and must be judged within its own context, which is not that of its source. The context of the Grail legend in Malory's treatment is the whole Arthurian story as treated by him. With his treatment of the Grail, Malory finally won his own limited independence of interpretation. From the end of the Grail story onwards there is hardly any need to argue the essential unity of Malory's great if simple conception. The seventh and eighth tales 'form together a coherent whole', as Professor Vinaver himself says (*W* lxxx; cf. xxxi).

The seventh tale comprises five adventures which show Lancelot at the precarious peak of his earthly fame, loving chivalry, 'Trouthe and honoure, fredom and curteisie'. These adventures culminate in the Healing of Sir Urry; at the end of this great passage, and of the whole tale, comes this final paragraph:

> And so I leve here of this tale, and overlepe grete bookis of sir Launcelot. . . . And because I have loste the very mater of Shevalere de Charyot I departe from the tale of sir Launcelot; and here I go unto the morte Arthur, and that caused sir Aggravayne (*W* 1154).

Malory's reference to 'Shevalere de Charyot' is something of a puzzle. Earlier (*W* 1130) he has told us that he has deliberately left off following 'La Shyvalere le Charyote', and in the final paragraph of the seventh tale (omitted for clarity in the quotation just made) he has told us briefly what happens in the 'grete bookis' he has 'overleapt'. So he had clearly read the great books, and was deliberately overleaping them. Perhaps when he says he has *lost* 'the very mater of Shevalere de Charyot' he means that it has been omitted—lost from the version he wishes to give us, because he is pressing on to more essential matters, as the *explicit* which follows the final paragraph explains:

> And here on the othir syde folowyth *The Moste Pyteuous Tale of the Morte Arthure Saunz Gwerdon* par le Shyvalere Sir Thomas Malleoré, Knyght (*W* 1154).

This *explicit* sends us straight on to the final instalment, the eighth and last tale, the *Morte Arthur* itself.[1] There is no specific bridge-passage at the beginning of this last tale, for as Professor Vinaver himself has observed, it forms a coherent whole with the preceding tale. But the first paragraph, about the month of May, ends by showing well enough how Malory conceived the larger movement which underlies the separate adventures:

> so thys season hit befelle in the moneth of May a grete angur and unhappy that stynted nat tylle the *floure of chyvalry of the worlde was destroyed and slayne*. (*W* 1161: italics mine.)

[1] Or as Professor Vinaver entitles it in his separate edition (Oxford, 1955), *The Tale of the Death of King Arthur*.

He has chronicled the rise and glory of the flower of chivalry of the world; now he comes to its grievous destruction.

The next paragraph tells how Agravain and Mordred were the immediate cause of the tragedy: but to understand even this demands our precedent knowledge of the whole long course of Lancelot's love for the Queen, of his greatness and pride, and of the more important greatness of Arthur, which nevertheless depends on Lancelot's loyalty. From this beginning of the eighth tale, of which the foundations have been laid so far back, the story moves forward surely and majestically, perhaps the first true tragedy in English, and one of the most moving. And it closes with a final *explicit*, which hammers home the essential unity of conception that has underlain the *whole book*:

> Here is the ende of the *hoole book* of kyng Arthur and of his noble knyghtes of the Rounde Table, that whan they were holé togyders there was ever an hondred and forty. And here is the ende of *The Deth of Arthur*. (*W* 1260: italics in l. 1 mine.)

Two things are finished; this particular tale, and the whole book of which it is part.[1]

The whole book is bound together in various ways: by the unity of atmosphere and the continuous moral concern; by the chronological continuity of the main events and characters (allowing for some overlapping in the *Launcelot*, *Gareth*, and *Tristram*, the central books where time is not so important); by significant references back and forward to important characters and events; and by links between the various tales. Some of this binding together is due to the inherent nature of Malory's material, and some of it to Malory's personal contribution. His method has been authoritatively described by Professor Vinaver; Malory has made

> (*a*) a rearrangement of episodes consistent with [his] own narrative technique, and (*b*) a series of connecting passages designed to link together the episodes so rearranged (*W* 1575).

But whereas Professor Vinaver would apply this only

[1] [Cf. p. 35 above.—Ed.]

within the eight major sections, we must also apply it to the book as a whole. Malory's method is the same both for the lesser arrangements within the tales, and for the major arrangements of the tales themselves. The smaller sections within the main tales correspond structurally to the major sections within the whole book. Often there are no close links between the subsections of a major tale; but no one doubts that they are parts of a larger whole. The subsections have a high degree of autonomy, just like the major sections.

Analogies for such a loose form as Malory devised are difficult to find, for the very good reason, as Professor Vinaver has shown, that Malory comes at an almost unique moment in the transition from late medieval to early modern methods of story-telling. Probably the closest analogy to Malory's form in English is found in *The Faerie Queene*. Spenser knew Malory's work, and it is possible that he understood Malory's form well enough. *The Faerie Queene* is vastly more subtle and learned than Malory, but it enables us to see how a series of stories may be linked only loosely together without much attempt at organic unity, and yet they must be regarded, as the six complete books of *The Faerie Queene* must be regarded, as one single work of art. Each work has an historical flavour, and each work owes its impression of cohesion to some extent to what may be called extra-aesthetic comments by the author. Thus our feeling about the cohesion of *The Faerie Queene* derives, to some extent, from the Letter to Raleigh, which is external to the poem proper, just as our feeling about the cohesion of *The Morte Darthur* derives to some slight extent from the *explicits*, which might not be regarded, by strict standards, as part of the artistic form.

One is bound to recognize Malory's lack of conscious artistry, his incapacity for abstract thought. But one must also recognize how difficult it was for him to extricate and clarify a coherent pattern from the cyclic tangle of his sources. His triumph lies especially in the last two books. Here the noble simplicity of theme, the moral earnestness, the firm conception of the roles of Lancelot and Arthur and Guinevere, the fertile invention of story and dialogue, the magnificent prose, all unite in a richness of feeling unparalleled in Arthurian literature before or since. Malory's genius is concrete, dramatic, moral; rooted in feeling, not in generalizing intellectual power. The greatness of his achievement lies in these last two tales, but they cannot be severed from the earlier books.

5

Chivalry in the *Morte*

P. E. TUCKER

[I]

THE purpose of this essay is to offer an interpretation of Malory's story of Lancelot, Guinevere, and Arthur, and to show that by means of this interpretation a satisfying view of the whole work may be gained. It involves a study of Malory's rejection of one ideal of chivalry (that of his French sources) and his gradual discovery of his own ideal. This process takes place chiefly in the history of Lancelot (it is the new *sens* developed in the given *matière*), but it can be discerned in almost every part of the work, and it binds the whole together. The most direct way of demonstrating this is by considering the nature of chivalry in the *Morte Darthur* —what it at first consists in, how it changes, and the originality of its final development. For chivalry is more than a nebulous term for the subject-matter of the work: it is an ideal of definite though changing content, the theme of all the stories which have been bound together. Moreover, it is probably the element that first attracted Malory to the Arthurian legend. To pursue this study it will be necessary to give some attention to the sources, in particular the Old French Arthurian prose romances, both for their general notions of chivalry and of love, and for precise details in Malory's re-writing. But we must also consider the few but crucial passages in which he comments on his story. These comments are usually oblique and difficult to interpret—he is at times a wayward and even a careless writer, and much depends upon the reader's willingness to treat the text sympathetically—but they are valuable indications of his drift. The *Morte Darthur* is remarkable for its gathering together of ancient material; its interest as an original work of great power is in the exploratory character of the author's writing, and in the final emergence of a new meaning for an old story.

In his book, *French chivalry* (Baltimore, 1940), Sidney Painter begins with a division of chivalry into three kinds —martial, courtly, and religious; and this will without further elaboration provide a convenient basis for a discussion of chivalry in the *Morte Darthur*. It is clear from the content of the first three books (of the Winchester MS.) that Malory's earliest interest was in the martial aspect of chivalry. This is most apparent in the *Tale of Arthur and Lucius*, the spirit of which derives directly from its source, the heroic alliterative *Morte Arthure*. But even here, and much more so in his re-writing of the French sources for the earlier books, Malory is not content merely to reproduce stories of deeds of arms. He tends to make additions and alterations which suggest, cumulatively, that his real interest was in the ideal he believed these stories exemplified. This ideal is not, at bottom, his own—he is in the first instance only exposing and magnifying certain notions that underlie his sources, such as the importance of sheer strength of arm and the aristocratic origin of chivalry. What is his own is the strong moral tone which pervades his accounts of chivalric conduct and makes its various aspects coalesce into a single sentiment.

Prowess is the first quality demanded of a knight, and Malory gives it particular prominence in his stories and comments. He describes single combats and tournaments in language more vigorous than that of his sources, sometimes adding details, and he takes special interest in the technique of fighting. One of his favourite phrases is 'a noble knight of prowess'. Apart from its inherent worth, prowess is admirable because it brings a knight reputation and honour, or what Malory calls 'worship'. Thus, in his treatment of the war waged by the Round Table in *The Tale of Arthur and Lucius* there is discernible a greater concern with the glory of the action than the original evinces (a difference of emphasis typical of the development of romantic chivalry out of the heroic poems). One of Arthur's comments on the action is typical of this view of the story: 'Be my fayth, there was never kynge sauff myselff that welded evir such knyghtes' (*W* 217). The effect of the whole Tale within the *Morte Darthur* is to suggest that the Round Table is the centre of the romances not merely by convention and for the convenient spinning of adventures, but because prowess and worship are there at their highest.

Malory also gives particular prominence to a code of conduct among knights. The true knight never takes his opponent unawares or fights him at a disadvantage, and although there is something boyish in this insistence on fair play, it is the earliest kind of courtesy associated with chivalry. Gawain, who in his first adventure causes the death of a lady when he is about to kill her protector, is reproved thus:

'Alas', seyde Gaherys, 'that ys fowle and shamefully done . . . ye sholde gyff mercy unto them that aske mercy, for a knyght withoute mercy ys withoute worship (*W* 106; not in source).

The code of conduct exemplified in the various adventures is summed up by Arthur in his charge to the Round Table at the end of Book I:

. . . Than the kynge stablysshed all the knyghtes and gaff them rychesse and londys: and charged them never to do outerage nothir morthir, and allwayes to fle treson, and to gyff mercy unto hym that askith mercy, uppon payne of forfiture of their worship and lordship of kynge Arthure for evirmore: and allwayes to do ladyes, damesels, and jantilwomen and wydowes socour: strengthe hem in hir ryghtes, and never to enforce them uppon payne of dethe. Also that no man take no batayles in a wrongefull quarell for no love ne for no worldis goodis (*W* 119–20; not in source).

There is remarkable fervour behind Malory's belief in chivalry, and its expression is often vehement:

'What?' seyde sir Launcelot. 'is he a theff and a knyght? And a ravyssher of women? He doth shame unto the Order of Knyghthode, and contrary unto his oth. Hit is pyté that he lyvyth!' (*W* 269; not in source).

The fervour derives from the fact that Malory sees knighthood as the outward expression of aristocracy, which he reverences. In his story of Torre, for example, the man of noble birth not only stands out from among the churls, but also shows his aptitude for arms even as a boy; and he will prove a good knight, Merlin says, for he is of good lineage. The refusal of Perceval and his brother to remain at home is the finest example of this view that knight-errantry is the natural obligation of noble birth:

'A, my swete modir, we may nat [abyde], for we be comyn of kynges bloode of bothe partis. And therefore, modir, hit ys oure kynde to haunte armys and noble dedys' (*W* 810; not in source).

In the early stages of Malory's writing, then, chivalry means prowess and the reputation that comes of prowess; it implies a standard of conduct or courtesy (which may develop into friendship and fellowship), and it is essentially artistocratic. These qualities are fused together in a sentiment which has the strength and fervour of a belief. No summary of its content can show the force of a belief, but it is noteworthy that if Malory's use of the terms 'chivalry', 'worship', and 'noble' is examined, their connotations are seen to merge into one another in a complex of meaning. It has already appeared that there is a peculiar virtue in prowess alone for Malory; it is admirable because it is something a knight must possess, something essential for worship or honour. The word 'worship' is used with this suggestion: 'There was never knyght dud more worshyp' (*W* 220); here it means primarily 'deeds of valour', but it has the connotations of glory and honour. It can also imply nobility: 'Manhode and worship ys hyd within a mannes person' (*W* 63). This is an aristocratic sentiment, for it is applied to Balin, who succeeds as a 'jantyll knyght' in drawing the damsel's sword in spite of his appearance. 'But for hys poure araymente she thought he sholde nat be of no worship withoute vylony or trechory' (*W* 63). 'Worship' and worshipful' are terms never applied to common people, and we find on the other hand that Arthur will 'dey a worshipfull dethe' (*W* 44); and again, 'Lat every man of worshyp florysh hys herte in thys worlde' (*W* 1119). The word 'chivalry' likewise has strong overtones, and the connotations of 'prowess' and 'worship': 'Than thoughte sir Launcelot for to helpe there the wayker party in incresyng of his shevalry', (*W* 931), i.e. his reputation for prowess as a knight. Knighthood is for Malory not only the outward expression of aristocratic nature, but also the highest type of excellence in a man, his worship.

This is plain and prosaic enough; the purpose of the foregoing is to emphasize Malory's veneration at the very beginning of his work for a particular kind of chivalry. He would call it 'pure knighthood', and it is a limited, austere ideal, quite distinct from the ideal of chivalry which he found in the French Arthurian prose romances, and of which Lancelot is the epitome. In these romances prowess and desire for reputation, nobility, courtesy, and friendship are all elements, but their outstanding and distinctive quality is the skill with which they make chivalric adventures the background for their treatment of love. 'Le but le plus ordinaire des prouesses chevaleresques', Albert Pauphilet wrote, 'est, comme on sait, la conquête de l'amour.'[1] The connexion between love and chivalry in Arthurian romances can be traced back to the primitive court of Arthur described by Geoffrey of Monmouth. It appears in his *Historia* as the simple suggestion that valour in arms may be increased by the desire to win love:

> Facetae enim mulieres . . . nullius amorem habere dignabantur nisi tertio in militia probatus esset. Efficiebantur ergo castae quaeque mulieres et milites pro amore illarum nobiliores[2]

Wace, when he translated Geoffrey into French, represented Gawain as the first of the courtly knights. Gawain says:

> Mult sunt bones les gaberies
> E bones sunt les druëries.
> Pur amistié e pur amies
> Funt chevaliers chevaleries.
> (*Brut*, vv. 10,769–72.)

But in Wace as in Geoffrey of Monmouth the primary justification for the pursuit of chivalry is still the desire for fame, and the glory of achievement alone. In Chrétien de Troyes the emphasis is altered, and chivalry becomes the pursuit in

[1] *Le legs du Moyen Age* (1950), p. 153.

[2] Sec. IX, ch. 13; from the text printed by E. Faral. J. Frappier, in quoting this passage, suggests that *facetae mulieres* may be interpreted as 'les dames courtoises': *Le roman breton* in *Les cours de Sorbonne*, 1951.

which above all a knight proves his fitness for love—so it may be said of Erec, Yvain, Lancelot. In the Prose *Lancelot* proper, 'courtly love' is a less rigorous code than in Chrétien's *Charrette*, and a great deal of space is given to martial episodes and to knightly adventures for their own sake, but the intimate connexion of love and chivalry remains and predominates. The centre of the work is Lancelot's love for Guinevere, in which every aspect of his knighthood is bound up: Lancelot, as the French writer makes Guinevere say, has accomplished all his exploits 'pour un seul mot'. The narrative illustrates this repeatedly, but it is best stated in Lancelot's own words to Guinevere:

'Sachies que ie ne fuisse ia uenus a si grant hautesce comme ie sui, se vous ne fuissies, quar iou neusse ia cuer de ma cheualerie encommencher ne demprendre lez coses que li autre laissoient par defaute de pooir. Mais ce que iou baoie a vous et a uostre tres grant biaute mist mon cuer en lorguel ou il estoit. Si que iou ne peusse trouuer nulle auenture que ie ne meisse bien a chief. Car iou sauoie bien se iou ne pooie passer les auentures par proece que a vous nauendroie iou ia. Et il me conuint auenir ou morir. Dont ie vous di uraiement que che estoit la chose qui plus acroissoit mes uertus.' (Sommer, *Vulgate Version of the Arthurian Romances.* (*V*, 193.)

Prowess and all the virtues of knighthood are inspired by love, and the service of love is their highest motive.

Malory's antipathy to this aspect of chivalry appears early in the *Morte Darthur*. In a version of the French *Merlin*, from which the *Tale of Arthur* is derived, he found first an account of the rise of Arthur and of his victorious wars against the other kings of Britain. This was entirely consonant with his interest in romance, and when later the court is established, and independent adventures begin, he is able to handle with equal competence such stories as that of *Balin and Balan*. The ideals involved, valour and defiance, are those that appeal to him, and the chief effect of his rehandling and abbreviating of the story is to give them greater emphasis. But when he comes to a story in which courtly sentiment is important, Malory gets into difficulties. For instance, in the French story of Pelleas and Ettard, Pelleas never falters in his devotion to his lady, even when he finds her asleep with Gawain, and ultimately they are united. Malory alters the events of the story, making Pelleas desert Ettard (who dies of love for him) and giving him the hand of Nyneve as a reward. In thus ignoring the courtly conventions of the original, and introducing a crude moral ending, Malory produces a not very coherent compromise, and this is the first of many compromises and confusions to follow.[1]

It is as regards the character of Lancelot, and in the first instance, in the *Tale of Sir Lancelot*, that the opposition between Malory's ideal of chivalry and that of his sources is fully exposed. Earlier, it appears, Malory had accepted Lancelot without question as the greatest exemplar of knighthood. He brought Lancelot to Arthur's court at the end of Book I, and in *The Tale of Arthur and Lucius* he seems to make alterations in order to present Lancelot as the leading knight of the Round Table; in that book, Lancelot exemplifies Malory's early ideals perfectly. But in Book III discordancy arises, and it may be deduced that Malory would have preferred to reject certain features of the character of Lancelot which his French sources now began to reveal. There is first some circumstantial evidence. Malory appears to have selected from his sources so as to produce a series of adventures in which Lancelot appears simply as the greatest of knights-errant; his love for Guinevere is mentioned, but it never forms the subject of the narrative. Of the three widely spaced sections from the French which form Malory's Book III as it now stands, each of the first two breaks off at a point where the narrative turns to Lancelot's adventures as a lover—namely, the story of Elaine and the quarrel with Guinevere, and the story of his capture by Morgan, who hopes that he will become her lover. Malory omits these episodes, but he omits little else that does not either include Guinevere or exclude Lancelot himself. It is true that one of these omissions, the story of Elaine, appears later in the *Morte Darthur*, but it is present almost by chance, an episode in the *Book of Sir Tristram*.

What makes it likely that Malory excluded the romantic

[1] [Cf. F. Whitehead's study of this story in *Medium Ævum* ii (1933), pp. 199–208.—Ed.]

episodes deliberately is the open appearance in this Book of his general distaste for courtly chivalry. There is a conversation between Lancelot and a damsel whom he has rescued which runs as follows:

'But one thyng, sir knyght, methynkes ye lak, ye that ar a knyght wyveles, that ye woll nat love som mayden other jantyl woman. For I cowde never here sey that ever ye loved ony of no maner of degré, and that is grete pyté. But hit is noysed that ye love quene Gwenyvere, and that she hath ordeyned by enchauntemente that ye shall never love none other but hir, nother none other damesell ne lady shall rejoyce you; wherefore there be many in this londe, of hyghe astate and lowe, that make grete sorow.'

'Fayre damesell,' seyde sir Launcelot, 'I may nat warne peple to speke of me what hit pleasyth hem. But for to be a weddyd man, I thynke hit nat, for than I must couche with hir and leve armys and turnamentis, batellys and adventures. And as for to sey to take my pleasaunce with peramours, that woll I refuse: in prencipall for drede of God, for knyghtes that bene adventures sholde nat be advoutrers nothir lecherous, for than they be nat happy nother fortunate unto the werrys: for other they shall be overcom with a sympler knyght than they be hemself, other ellys they shall sle by unhappe and hir cursednesse bettir men than they be hemself. And so who that usyth peramours shall be unhappy, and all thynge unhappy that is aboute them' (*W* 270–71).

In the style of Lancelot's speech here appear both the vehemence which has already been mentioned as an expression of Malory's fervour for a moral ideal of chivalry, and the equally characteristic awkwardness, even ambiguity, of his general comments. The damsel tells Lancelot that he ought as a knight to be a lover; he replies that his notion of chivalry takes no account of love, even deliberately excludes it. This dialogue has usually been felt to need elucidation, and it has been suggested that Lancelot is concealing his love for Guinevere in order to protect her reputation.[1] In this way some appearance of consistency might be preserved in Malory's presentation of Lancelot, but the motive attributed to Lancelot is too subtle for this stage of Malory's work. The manner in which the real question, the relation of Lancelot to Guinevere, is avoided, and the vehemence with

[1] Cf. R. T. Davies, 'Malory's "Vertuouse love",' *Studies in Philology* liii (1956), p. 460.

which 'love of paramours' is censured, suggest together that Malory himself is irritated by the matter; and this interpretation is borne out by other passages in which he rejects some of the courtly assumptions and conventions of his sources.

It will be objected that Malory has already, before this dialogue, presented Lancelot as the lover of Guinevere. He mentions Merlin's warning to Arthur on Guinevere's marriage, and at the beginning of Book III he says explicitly:

> So this sir Launcelot encresed so mervaylously in worship and honoure . . . Wherefore quene Gwenyvere had hym in grete favoure aboven all other knyghtis, and so he loved the quene agayne aboven all other ladyes dayes of hys lyff, and for hir he dud many dedys of armys and saved her from the fyre thorow his noble chevalry (*W* 253).

Clearly Malory knew that Lancelot was traditionally the lover of Guinevere. The explanation of the inconsistency lies in Malory's carelessness—sometimes he reproduces the ideas of his sources, sometimes he corrects them or protests against them—and above all in the haphazard way in which he made the *Morte Darthur*: his interpretation of his material developed as he progressed. He took Lancelot as the exemplar of chivalry—his own conception of chivalry—and without thinking of the outcome, gladly reproduced the association of his name with Guinevere's because it heightened his glory. Only when it was openly suggested that a knight ought to be a lover did Malory realize the implications of the character he had given Lancelot, for he did not really believe that all his virtues were inspired by and existed for love. Ultimately, Malory discovered that he might present Lancelot and Guinevere as lovers while at the same time condemning the relationship as unworthy of Lancelot's knighthood, and this is the new *sens* which he wrote into the *matière* of the Lancelot story.

[II]

The argument presented above can be reinforced by a consideration of Malory's *Book of Sir Tristram*. This will show in greater detail what it is that Malory dislikes in the tradition of courtly chivalry, and show also his first attempt to express his own ideals of love.

For this book Malory's source-material was less coherent. In the French Prose *Tristan* the love-intrigue does not play so important a part as it does in the Prose *Lancelot*; chivalric adventures, as the other hand, are given more room. Thus, one defect of Malory's version, that the love-story is not placed firmly at the centre of interest, is to be traced in part to the original. Yet the French romance still accommodates the love-story easily, and it still sees the pursuit of love as a natural part of knight-errantry. Malory accepts the necessity of having a knight-lover as hero, but his lack of sympathy with the story almost destroys it. (He seems scarcely aware that by persistently selecting and altering in small particulars he is reshaping his material and so beginning to create a different impression of the meaning of the story.) On the other hand, he begins to show what kind of love is acceptable to him. It appears, gradually, that he believes strongly in natural—that is, unsophisticated—love and fidelity; but these ideals, later so important, do not harmonize very well with the story he is at present trying to tell.

It seems at the very outset that Malory is more interested in Tristram as a martial hero than in his love for Isode. For instance, early in the narrative there is a hint that Tristram would gladly give up the company of Isode and join Lancelot in his exploits, if he could. Later Malory sends the lovers away to the forest somewhat abruptly, and he omits completely the French account of their life there together. When Tristram goes to Brittany his new relationship with Isode le Blanche Maynes is quickly explained, and his forsaking of the first Isode glossed over. (' . . . Sir Trystrames had suche chere and ryches and all other plesaunce that he had allmoste forsakyn La Beale Isode.') The source makes it clear that Tristan could never forget the first Isode, and that he was led into marriage with the other by accident. Malory's own statement, that Tristram could not endure without Isode, is not made plausible. On the other hand, much is made of Tristram's other virtues as a knight. He is famed for his prowess and courtesy, and skilled in the aristocratic pastime of hunting. His career culminates in the welcome he is given at Arthur's court, of which the importance is magnified by Malory. An impression is created that it is his worship as a knight rather than his love for Isode which entitles him to possess her, for he tells King Mark that he is ill-rewarded for his services to Cornwall in being deprived of her, and when he believes she is false his first reaction is to recall that 'mony londis and grete rychesse have I forsakyn for youre love'.

Tristram's relations with the other characters show the same tendency in Malory to push the love-intrigue into the background. The role of King Mark is significant in this respect. He is treated as a complete villain, not so much for his enmity of the lovers as for his unchivalrous treatment of Tristram's person. He is the enemy of all good knights, but where in the French we find Palomides, for instance, making fun of him, in Malory he speaks in a serious moral tone:

'A, false knyght! . . . hit ys pité thou haste thy lyff, for thou arte a destroyer of all worshipfull knyghtes, and by thy myschyff and thy vengeaunce thou haste destroyed that moste noble knyght, sir Trystramys de Lyones . . .' (*W* 497).

Palomides is given an important role in Malory's version. At first he and Tristram meet and fight for the love of Isode, but as Palomides comes under the influence of Tristram's courtesy he gives up his love. In the French he is more than once found soliloquizing, trying to justify his hopeless love by the reflection that it encourages all kinds of virtue in him. This kind of traditional courtly sentiment is omitted in Malory, and instead we find Palomides calling himself foolish to love Isode when 'the beste knyght of the worlde' loves her. It is significant that the Book ends with a great combat and final reconciliation between Tristram and Palomides; and Palomides agrees to be christened for the sake of his friendship, not for the love of Isode. No such reconciliation appears in the French versions; it is possible in Malory because it was the rivalry of two noble knights that mattered, not the cause of it. So Segwarides, Tristram's rival in another love-affair, can say, 'I woll never hate a noble knyght for a lyght lady' (*W* 442).

There are many other omissions and alterations in the

Book of Sir Tristram. The general effect is to make the interest in chivalry alone so predominant that the love-story —itself inadequately told—loses its essential dependence on its setting; and this is of all love-stories perhaps the one that becomes most meaningless when isolated from its context of unusual conventions. From what has so far been examined of Malory's writing it appears that a knight need not have a lady, but if he takes one he takes no more than his due reward. His declarations that he is her servant are no more than a polite fiction, for his real business is the disinterested pursuit of knight-errantry. Fortunately for the rest of his work, Malory was not satisfied with this meagre representation of Arthurian romance, but it will be necessary to consider yet another of his protests before his more positive notions become clear.

In the middle of the *Tristram* Book, Mark is taken to task for his treatment of Tristram:

Sir Percivale . . . told the kynge that he had done hymselff grete shame for to preson sir Trystram so, 'for he is now the knyght of moste reverence in the worlde lyvynge, and wyte you well that the noblyste knyghtes of the worlde lovyth sir Trystram. And yf he woll make warre uppon you, ye may nat abyde hit.'

'That is trouthe,' seyde kynge Marke, 'but I may nat love sir Trystram, bycause he lovyth my quene, La Beall Isode.'

'A, fy for shame,' seyde sir Percivale, 'sey ye never so more! For ar nat ye uncle unto sir Trystram? And by youre neveaw ye sholde never thnyke that so noble a knyght as sir Trystram is, that he wolde do hymselff so grete vylany to holde his unclys wyff. Howbehit . . . he may love youre quene synles, because she is called one of the fayryst ladyes of the worlde' (*W* 679; from *And by* not in source).

'Holde' here seems to mean not simply possess, but possess physically, a special sense of 'love'. The *O.E.D.* cites for this meaning a line in the *Destruction of Troy*: 'Pirrus . . . Weddit that worthi & as wif held.' Elsewhere in the *Morte Darthur* the same sense is present in Agravain's speech to Arthur: 'We know all that sir Launcelot holdith youre quene, and hath done longe . . .' made at a time when Guinevere is not actually in Lancelot's keeping. Arthur later accuses Lancelot in the same terms (*W* 1163, 1187). Perceval seems to say, then, that Tristram is too noble a knight ever to stoop to adultery, and yet, he adds, if he loves Isode he is not to be blamed, for she is beautiful. This comment cannot very easily be attributed to Perceval dramatically. It would be out of place, for the speaker has no developed character in the book, and it is the kind of comment no author would insert unless he intended to develop it—for it is a criticism of the central feature of the story. Malory was perfectly aware of the relation between Tristram and Isode; he relates how 'sir Trystram was takyn nakyd abed wyth La Beall Isode' early in the story (*W* 431), and how Palomides 'wyste well that sir Trystram enjoyed her' (*W* 615)—and it is to this relationship that Mark refers. Yet when the accusation is brought into the open (in a context where he has begun by describing Tristram as the noblest of knights) Malory cannot allow the admission that he is an adulterer. The final remark, 'he may love youre quene synles, because she is called one of the fayryst ladyes of the worlde' might be taken to mean that Tristram is justified in his adultery because Isode is beautiful. This is the kind of justification that lies behind Lancelot's love for Guinevere in the French tradition. It is alien to Malory's notions, but it would not have been impossible for him to have repeated it as an excuse for Tristram. However, it makes better sense in the context of the story if we understand Perceval to say that it is not improper for Tristram to love Isode from a distance (as Palomides does).

This raises the question whether Malory at heart believes only in love free from sensual desire, as some writers on the *Morte Darthur* have suggested or implied. Malory occasions this belief when he writes of Lancelot's visit to Guinevere's bedchamber:

> For, as the Freynshhe booke seyth, the quene and sir Launcelot were togydirs. And whether they were abed other at other maner of disportis, me lyste nat thereof make no mencion, for love that tyme was nat as love ys nowadayes (*W* 1165).

As Professor Vinaver points out, the report of the English source ('to bede he gothe with the quene') and that of the French ('se coucha avec la roïne') are carefully avoided. Professor R. H. Wilson adduces the following passage:

For men and women coude love togydirs seven yerys, and no lycoures lustis was betwyxte them, and than was love, trouthe and faythefulness. And so in lyke wyse was used such love in kynge Arthurs dayes (*W* 1120).

He interprets this as an advocacy of 'platonic love', and suggests that Lancelot's outburst to the damsel against love carries the same implication.[1] It is possible that Malory imagined (or hoped) for a time that the 'courtly love' of his sources did not embrace sensual desire, but he must quickly have become aware of the real nature of love in King Arthur's days. Early in the *Morte Darthur* there are passages that make this certain. Gawain and Ettard (in the story mentioned above) 'wente to bedde togedyrs', and in another story dame Lyonesse came to Gareth's bed, 'And there-withall he began to clyppe hir and to kysse hir'. In the *Tristram* Book Malory describes plainly the physical relation between the lovers, and he does not really deceive himself over Lancelot and Guinevere. In the *Knight of the Cart* he writes:

So, to passe uppon thys tale, sir Launcelot wente to bedde with the quene and toke no force of hys hurte, but toke hys pleasaunce and hys lykynge untyll hit was the dawnyng of the day; for wyte you well, he slept nat, but wacched' (*W* 1131).

—and in the later part of the story there is no possibility of doubt. Love was not 'platonic' in Arthur's time, and it is not even necessary to believe that this kind of love was Malory's ideal; the apparent evidence for it can be better interpreted, and on the other hand Malory shows elsewhere that he has other notions.

In the story of Lancelot and Elaine, Malory tells how Dame Brisen brought Lancelot to Elaine's bed.

And wyte you well this lady was glad, and so was sir Launcelot, for he wende that he had had another in hys armys.

Now leve we them kyssynge and clyppynge *as was a kyndely thynge* . . . (*W* 804–5).

This behaviour is a 'natural thing', a phrase that Malory appears to have added himself. In the French we find:

[1] 'Characterization in Malory', pp. 50ff.; a copy of this dissertation (v. *W* 1658, no. 89) is deposited in the Bodleian Library.

. . . chil se couche de les lui, et cele le rechoit a grant ioie, et il li fait autel soulas et autel ioie comme il auoit a coustume a faire a sa dame la roïne, car il·quidoit uraiement que che fust ele. En tel ioie et en tel deduit sendorment cil dune part et cele dautre, et se tint cascuns a boin eure, cil de sa dame que il quide tenir, et cele del home del monde que ele plus aime. . . . (Text from the relevant section of the Prose *Tristan* transcribed by H. O. Sommer in *Modern Philology* v (1907–8), p. 79.)

Malory's distaste is not so much for the physical part of love as for a sophisticated account of it. He dislikes the way in which his sources seem to make a cult of love, and although he often merely reproduces what is before him he is sometimes provoked into a protest, in which he may say more than he means. The conversation between Lancelot and the damsel is an instance of this, and there Malory's dislike of what he would consider the immoral aspect of love is apparent. A great deal is said of 'love of paramours'. The meaning of the word 'paramour' is itself difficult to delimit precisely, but for Malory it almost always implies a sexual relation outside marriage. He is inclined to insist on the distinction between marriage and 'love paramours', setting them over against one another. Thus Arthur asks Gareth 'whether he wolde have this lady as peramour, other ellys to have hir to wyff', and the relation between Lancelot and the Maid of Astolat is described with the same directness:

'Sir, I wolde have you to my husbande.'

'Fayre damesell, I thanke you hartely, but truly I caste me never to be wedded man.'

'Than, fayre knyght, woll ye be my paramour?'

'Jesu deffende me! For than I rewarded youre fadir and youre brothir full evyll for their grete goodnesse' (*W* 1089).

As Professor Vinaver points out, 'Any suggestion of a marriage being arranged between Lancelot and the Maid of Astolat would be unthinkable in the French romance'. But to Malory it is proper that the Maid should marry, and he even makes Lancelot offer to establish her with 'som good knyght' by a gift of money. Malory dislikes the notion of 'love paramours', because it implies mere pleasure-taking. When he describes how Lancelot met Elaine, and how

Galahad was conceived, he shows more carefully than the French version that Lancelot was under enchantment when he lay with Elaine, he elaborates the explanations of his source, and he emphasizes Lancelot's shame. He also makes Elaine's love for Lancelot more important, chiefly by making her see Guinevere as an obstacle to her marriage with him. In all this may be seen his desire to remove any suggestion of 'love of paramours'.

To Malory the 'courtly love' of his sources seemed artificial and cultivated for its own sake, and to judge from one alteration, he felt that the French often slurred over what was immoral with a show of fair words. In a short episode in the French *Tristan* Persides tells how he was solicited by a lady. The tone is courtly: 'La dame me uit biel che li fu auis quele me requist damors, et iou li dis que iou nen feroie rien se ele ne sen uenoit od moi, et ele le me creanta.' Malory describes the encounter more plainly, and he makes Persides refuse: 'And therein dwellyth an uncurteyse lady, and . . . she proffyrd me to be her paramoure, and I refused her' (*W* 813). The courteous lady has become discourteous, and when Perceval himself comes to the castle he rebukes her thus:

'A madame, what use and custom ys that in a lady to destroy good knyghtes but yf they woll be youre paramour? Perdé, this is a shameful custom of a lady . . .' (*W* 814).

This passage is not in the French, and it again shows Malory's moral disapproval. Love should be spontaneous, and the outcome of natural affection—that of the Maid of Astolat is the pattern for Malory. In his version of her story (in which he is completely successful in imposing a new *sens* on the original material) the conversations lose all courtly locutions, and the Maid's manner becomes not cruder but simply bolder and more natural. The change is most striking in her last words, when she justifies herself:

'Why sholde I leve such thoughtes? Am I nat an erthely woman? . . . My belyve ys that I do none offence, though I love an erthely man, unto God, for He fourmed me thereto, and all maner of good love comyth of God . . .' (*W* 1093).

The whole speech is simple, direct, and passionate. Lancelot's justification for his part is made equally clear when he tells the queen:

'Madame, she wolde none other wayes be answerde but that she wolde be my wyff, othir ellis my paramour. and of thes two I wolde not graunte her . . . For, madame, I love nat to be constrayned to love, for love muste only aryse of the harte selff, and nat by none constraynte' (*W* 1097).

This is the ideal that first begins to develop in the *Book of Sir Tristram*, even in the intractable and finally abandoned story of Tristram and Isode. There are various apparent alterations which show Malory trying to suggest in Isode the same kind of natural affection. We find, for instance, that her first love for Tristram is boldly expressed, especially at their parting in Ireland, and in the fine recognition scene after Tristram's madness she speaks in a tone very different from that of the traditional mistress of courtly love:

'And ever whan I may I shall sende unto you, and whan ye lyste ye may com unto me, and at all tymes early and late I woll be at youre commaundement, to lyve as poore a lyff as ever ded quyene or lady' (*W* 502).

Together with natural affection in love Malory prizes fidelity on both sides. His Beaumairis rejects completely the courtly tradition that a knight should remain unmoved by his mistress's infidelity or disdain—'to love that lovyth nat the is but grete foly' (*W* 322). Later, when Lancelot and Guinevere are admitted to be lovers fidelity is fully maintained and praised as an ideal. It is noteworthy that Malory's *Tale of the Sankgreal* contains no condemnation of Guinevere, such as that found in the French *Queste del Saint Graal*, and at the end of his reflections on love in *The Knight of the Cart* he writes of Guinevere that 'whyle she lyved she was a trew lover, and therefor she had a good ende'. He seems here to be implying that Guinevere (though imperious in her treatment of Lancelot) remained faithful to him until there could be no more faith of lovers, and then she died a religious death.

This passage, which ends with a 'lytyll mencion' of Guinevere, is the most important of Malory's comments on the story. It is concerned largely with stability, that is, loyalty in love:

> But nowadayes men can nat love sevennyght but they muste have all their desyres. That love may nat endure by reson, for where they bethe sone accorded and hasty, heete sone keelyth. And ryght so faryth the love nowadayes, sone hote sone colde. Thys ys no stabylyté. But the olde love was nat so. For men and women coude love togydirs seven yerys, and no lycoures lustis was betwyxte them, and than was love, trouthe, and faythefulnes. And so in lyke wyse was used such love in kynge Arthurs dayes (*W* 1119–20).

There is no necessity to construe this as an advocacy of 'platonic' love. The general complaint is against those who cannot remain loyal in love, and Malory speaks in particular of the hasty and fickle spirit which cannot establish affection before desiring satisfaction. In Arthur's time men and women kept faith for long years; there was love, truth, and fidelity between them, but no wanton lust. Malory finds fidelity in love praiseworthy in itself—ultimately, perhaps, because it is a form of loyalty.

However, this is to anticipate Malory's full account of the love of Lancelot and Guinevere. At the end of the main part of the *Book of Sir Tristram* he appears to be left with the problem of how to treat that story—how he is to present Lancelot, the pattern of knightly virtue, as an adulterer with his sovereign's wife. In his French source there is no incompatibility here; Malory wants to show an incompatibility, and to show it not in isolated and incongruous outbursts of protest, but in an harmonious reinterpretation of the whole story of the fall of the Round Table. At this time he was perhaps hardly even aware of the nature of the difficulty before him. The solution to the problem was to emerge almost incidentally in his attempt to re-write the *Queste del Saint Graal*; but before turning to that it will be worth while to glance at the completely separate episode in the *Book of Sir Tristram*, the story of Elaine.

There is evidence here of the manner in which Malory might have completed the rest of his work. He might have partially retold the story of Lancelot and Guinevere just as he has partially retold Elaine's story and have been moderately successful without achieving the masterliness of the last sections of the *Morte Darthur*. In Malory's version we have a finer and more human presentation of the two chief characters: Elaine makes her declaration of love to Lancelot with the directness of Isode and the Maid of Astolat, and Lancelot's greatness as a knight is heightened by touches of vigour and pathos in the prose recounting his exploits and experiences—he begins for the first time to become a distinct human figure. Moreover, the whole story evidences Malory's increasing skill in creating a well-defined section of narrative within a larger framework—it is terser and better-knit than its source (though the comparison is not altogether fair to the different narrative aims of the French author). Yet in spite of these merits the story never rises fully to the possibilities of its subject. Lancelot is ashamed and humiliated in love, but Malory is saved from having to cope with what was for him the real difficulty in Lancelot's character—the pull of two incompatible codes—by the elimination of any factor of choice. For the obvious infidelity here is not in Lancelot's relation with Guinevere, but in his relation with Elaine. The already existing infidelity does not arise in the French, and Malory does not mention it; the other is covered by the fact that Lancelot sleeps with Elaine under the spell of enchantment. Malory makes the enchantment more prominent, but it could be no more than a provisional substitute for independence of character in Lancelot. Yet the story is well told, and it can be read as part of the history of Lancelot; it has the value, moreover, of introducing in connexion with Lancelot, however vaguely and tentatively, some foreshadowing of a novel force behind events in the Arthurian world—the mystery of the Grail.

[III]

In his 1929 monograph on Malory, Professor Vinaver compared *The Tale of the Sankgreal* with its source, and came to the conclusion that Malory had failed to re-create the meaning of the original; he had produced 'a confused and almost pointless story, a beautiful parade of symbols and bright visions'. In the edition of the *Works* this verdict is changed only to allow that in Malory's *Quest* Lancelot 'develops into something like a living character', and in the main this book is judged as a translation. A different approach is adopted in an essay entitled 'Malory and the Grail Legend' by the late Charles Williams.[1] He accepts Malory's *Quest* as an independent work (which is the first essential), and to show its significance in the *Morte Darthur* he examines the relation between Lancelot and Galahad, attempting to find a link between the opposed ideals of love and religion. This is a suggestive piece of criticism, but in fact Malory never shows that he is aware of or seeking for any mystic significance in this relationship. It can be maintained that Professor Vinaver is too closely influenced by the French text, and that Charles Williams escapes too easily from Malory's. Malory did fail to understand the theology of the French *Queste* (which is of fundamental importance in it), but his chief interest is the story of Lancelot, as both critics realize, and his version gains coherence if it is seen as concerned, however confusedly, with Lancelot's experience.

The French *Queste del Saint Graal* is a strict allegory in which the chivalric adventures of the Round Table knights are interpreted as symbols in a pilgrimage, an interpretation facilitated by the conception of man's life as a spiritual warfare. The Quest is a search for divine grace through a clearly defined Christian discipline, that of the Cistercians, and the Grail itself is the symbol of grace, finally achieved in the beatific vision. Many aspects of Christian life and doctrine are alluded to in the *Queste*, but the writer is chiefly concerned not with dogma and philosophy but with virtuous conduct (which opens a way for the operations of grace). In particular he deals with sensuality. This is the cardinal sin of 'courtly love', and the impression is given that a large part of the purpose of the work was to condemn the ideals of 'courtly love' as they existed at Arthur's court in the prose romances, and to substitute religious ones. The opposition between chastity and sensuality is exemplified in

[1] *The Dublin Review* April 1944, pp. 144–53.

the contrast between Galahad and Lancelot, and further illustrated in the adventures of Bors. Thus two ways of life are opposed, one secular and evil, described as 'worldly chivalry', the other religious, the way of 'celestial chivalry'. The way of worldly chivalry, which the Round Table knights had led before the Quest began, also involved another sin, homicide, but it was above all the evil life of the knight who is a lover. Not that the French author makes specific mention of 'love paramours': he assumes that it is bound up with the pursuit of earthly chivalry.

Inevitably Malory was confused by the two senses of 'chivalry' in the French *Queste*. In the first place, chivalry had no courtly implications for him, and it was in itself a high moral ideal. He was therefore at a loss to understand why the French writer persistently condemned *la chevaillierie terriene*, quite apart from his difficulty in grasping the exact nature of *la chevaillierie celestiale*. For, in the second place, he did not follow the theological expositions of his source, and the result was that he never fully grasped the purpose of the *Queste*. His translation follows his procedure in the *Tristram* Book; in general he reproduces what he has before him, making careless mistakes that reveal a lack of sympathy with what he is writing, but where the ideas of his material contradict his own too strongly, he makes alterations. These alterations arise from his preoccupation with his own ideal of chivalry and from his belief that Lancelot is far from being completely evil. They appear at first to be quite arbitrary, but they certainly do not shield Lancelot at all costs from judgement, and slowly there emerges from them a fairly coherent and acceptable impression of the meaning of Lancelot's experience in the Quest. Herein Malory discovers how to reconcile the interest of his material in courtly chivalry with his own ideal of 'pure knighthood'. He does this quite simply by taking the censure of chivalry in the *Queste* as an attack only upon its courtly aspect, a distinction in which the French writer is not interested. Thus, the whole weight of the Grail influence (which is discernible in his version after the Quest itself is over) is made to serve his own moral intention, crudely at first, then with increasing skill and conviction.

Lancelot's first important 'adventure' in the Quest is his dream and humiliation at the chapel (*W* 894ff.; *C* XIII. 18–19). His complaint when he wakes up in a state of misery and desolation reveals Malory's concern with what may be called for the moment secular standards of conduct:

'My synne and my wyckednes hath brought me unto grete dishonoure! For whan I sought worldly adventures for worldely desyres I ever encheved them and had the bettir in every place, and never was I discomfite in no quarell, were hit ryght were hit wronge. And now I take uppon me the adventures to seke of holy thynges, now I se and undirstonde that myne olde synne hyndryth me and shamyth me, that I had no power to stirre nother speke whan the holy bloode appered before me' (*W* 896).

(Here in the original version Lancelot reflects on his state of mortal sin, and he does not recall his failings in chivalry.) Shortly afterwards he makes his confession to a hermit:

And than he tolde there the good man all hys lyff, and how he had loved a quene unmesurabely and oute of mesure longe.

'And all my grete dedis of armys that I have done for the moste party was for the quenys sake, and for hir sake wolde I do batayle *were hit ryght other wronge*. And never dud I batayle all only for Goddis sake, but for to wynne worship and to cause me the bettir to be beloved, and litill or nought I thanked never God of hit' (*W* 897).

Here even more explicit reference is made to a distinction between right and wrong conduct in chivalry. For the French writer this distinction in worldly chivalry was irrelevant; to Malory, Lancelot's fault is that for the sake of Guinevere he had neglected in his quarrels standards of right and wrong, which he should have placed above all other considerations. This distinction is reinforced by the suggestion that Lancelot all too often fought 'to wynne worship and to cause me the bettir to be beloved'. Later, he is told as if by God:

'I have loste all that I have besette in the, for thou hast ruled the ayenste me as a warryoure and used wronge warris with vayneglory for the pleasure of the worlde more than to please me . . .' (*W* 928).

His faults are vainglory and pride, and his pursuit of them

was sinful. This pride of the warrior is quite distinct from the pride condemned in the French text, which is presumed to arise from lust, not from chivalry, and Malory draws upon it again most effectively in the story of the fall of the Round Table.

Lancelot's last important adventure before he meets Galahad is a tournament. Two parties of knights engage, one black and one white. Lancelot tries to help the losing party (the black), but in spite of his efforts they are defeated, and he himself is led off to follow a different direction. In the French the whole incident is a careful and skilful allegory. We learn that the two parties represent the sin-stained knights of the Round Table (*li chevalier terrien*) and the true knights (*li chevalier celestiel*) exemplified by Galahad, Perceval, and Bors. Lancelot had enlisted first on the side of the sinners in the Quest, but after his humiliation he had been shown a new way. Malory does not properly appreciate the purpose of this episode, and his version is a curious mingling of ideas ineffectually reproduced from the French, and of an attempt to relate and interpret the incident in his own fashion. To the French writer the adventure is an allegorical representation of Lancelot's previous experience in the Quest, a recapitulation of his spiritual progress. To Malory the tournament is important as a real event and a real lesson for Lancelot:

> Than thoughte sir Launcelot for to helpe there the wayker party *in incresyng of his shevalry* (*W* 931).

The recluse tells him to beware of the fault of 'bobbaunce and pryde of the worlde'. The general implication again is that 'good chivalry' as Malory understands it is acceptable to God, a notion quite intelligible in itself, and one that will become important in the sequel.

Again, in the French version of this episode Lancelot is reproached for his lack of faith; his regret for the old way of life (when he never suffered such defeats) symbolizes a failure to trust in God's guidance during his spiritual progress. This failure runs all through the French account of Lancelot in the Quest, and it is contrasted with the absolute trust of Galahad. Malory makes something different of this, partly, at least, because he did not realize the doctrinal importance of absolute faith. In interpreting the tournament he emphasizes Lancelot's lack of trust, but the interest is rather in a fault of character than in a point of Christian doctrine. Lancelot is not so much lacking in faith as unstable; his resolution is weak, so that he can neither endure the discipline of the Quest nor banish all other thoughts from his mind. Albert Pauphilet suggests that Lancelot is typical of the ordinary man who stumbles daily from errors to repentance, and for whom the confessors and preachers of the Church chiefly exist—'âme trébuchante et chancelante, à qui il faut des conseils continuels et une règle étroite'.[1] But the French *Queste* does not really present a Lancelot wavering and unstable, who keeps falling back into sin; each confession simply intensifies the impression of the preceding one, and there is no marked back-sliding between them. Pauphilet's description might more aptly be applied to Malory's Lancelot, whose submission to the discipline of the Quest is less perfect. The difference between the two presentations of Lancelot, in this respect, is well illustrated by the events that follow the tournament and its interpretation in each version. In the French version Lancelot leaves the recluse and rides until he reaches a deserted prominence, where he spends the night in solitary prayer. When he rides on he resigns himself to being unhorsed by a black knight, and at the end of the day again makes his submission in prayer. When the marvellous ship arrives, he waits on it patiently, and is again confessed. In these passages, which describe the climax of Lancelot's endeavour, the character whom Pauphilet describes is no longer visible. Malory's Lancelot labours in the discipline, but at this very point, the vigil on the ship, his strength of purpose fails:

So with thys jantillwoman (the dead sister of Perceval) sir Launcelot was a moneth and more . . . And so on a nyght he wente to play hym by the watirs syde, for he was somwhat wery of the shippe (*W* 1011–12).

This has been regarded as a short-coming in Malory; but

[1] *Études sur la Queste del Saint Graal attribuée à Gautier Map* (Paris, 1921) p. 130.

we may accept the incident as a genuine expression of Lancelot's weakness.

In these alterations Malory provides a reason for the failure of Lancelot to achieve the Quest of the Grail in the fullest sense. There is something paradoxical about Lancelot's quest, in the French as in Malory, for he both succeeds and fails in it. The vision he is granted is only partial, inferior to that of Galahad and Perceval. In the French it seems that his partial success is a reward for the penance he has undergone, and his failure (which is much more strongly marked) is due to his lack of absolute faith—for instance, he draws his sword at the guarded gates of the Grail castle. To Malory it must have seemed strange that Lancelot, after the intense penance to which he submits in the French version, should so easily be denied the achievement of Galahad. In his own version an explanation for this is still necessary, for even though much of the censure Lancelot receives in the French is omitted, he still undergoes trials and humiliations and does penance. Indeed, while the French writer seems to degrade Lancelot systematically, Malory makes him accept his penance more willingly. In the adventure at the Chapel he failed 'to ryse agayne the holy vessell' but (in Malory's addition) 'he toke repentaunce aftir that'. Later there is a conversation between some of the fellowship about success in the Quest in which they wonder what has befallen Lancelot, Galahad, Perceval, and Bors:

'Lette hem be', seyde sir Gawayne, 'for they four have no peerys. And if one thynge were nat, sir Launcelot he had none felow of an erthely man: but he ys as we be, but if he take the more payne uppon hym' (*W* 941; first sentence only in source).

Lancelot is no better than the others, *unless* he undertakes greater trials. To Malory it was plain that Lancelot does strive harder than any other knight, and that he suffers greater humiliations; that is why he so nearly achieves the Grail. The reason for his relative failure is the one already suggested, that in spite of his desire his will is not strong enough. 'And nere were that he ys nat stable, but by hys thoughte he ys lyckly to turne agayne, he sholde be nexte to encheve hit sauff sir Galahad . . .' (*W* 948; not in source). Lancelot's instability undoes all his submission and penance. Hence Malory's frequent description of Lancelot as at once the best of knights and a sinful man. The insistence on Lancelot's greatness is constantly tempered in this way. Thus:

'Now have I warned the of thy vayneglory and of thy pryde, that thou haste tyme arred ayenste thy Maker. Beware of everlastynge payne, for of all erthly knyghtes I have moste pité of the, for I know well thou haste nat thy pere of ony erthly synfull man.' (*W* 934; last part not in source.)

The description is a two-edged one that implies at once his success and his failure.

It would perhaps be impossible to decide whether Lancelot's instability of purpose is derived directly from his inner reservations during the Quest, but this is what the story as a whole implies. It is said that 'By hys thoughte he ys lyckly to turne agayne', and we deduce from the sequel that this refers to his inability to banish thoughts of Guinevere from his mind, as he was adjured by the hermits. This motive is totally absent from the French version, and is perhaps the most important in Malory's. Lancelot's later apologies and reproaches to Guinevere make it perfectly clear:

'And if that I had nat had my prevy thoughtis to returne to youre love agayne as I do, I had sene as grete mysteryes as ever saw my sonne sir Galahad, Percivale, other sir Bors' (*W* 1046).

The connexion between lack of resolution and lack of whole-hearted dedication to the Quest is again suggested when, after the fall of the Round Table, Guinevere tells Lancelot that she cannot believe that he will find the strength of will to stay in monastic life; he will 'turn to the world again'. Possibly the French writer's notion of lack of faith in Lancelot gave Malory a hint for the development of this 'instability', but as a trait of character, and as an element of major importance in the later story of Lancelot, it is Malory's own invention. The falling-off of Lancelot in Book VII is perfectly anticipated by Malory in the message that Galahad sends when Lancelot, grateful and (it seems) a litte proud of what he has achieved, has returned to Camelot—'Salew me unto my lorde sir Launcelot, my fadir, and as sone as ye se hym bydde hym remembir of this worlde unstable' (*W* 1035; the last part not in source).

The final scene, in which Lancelot receives this message, and the knights of the Quest are back at Camelot, is largely the invention of Malory. This conclusion is important, because it shows clearly how he envisaged the Quest. In his version there is no sense of finality, no implication that an earlier way of life has been superseded. The Quest, in short, has not broken the Round Table. It was rather a special discipline for the knights from which they must necessarily return to Camelot: the daily life of chivalry has still to be lived. This conception explains why the French scale of values undergoes a change in Malory, and why he appears to be 'secularizing' the Quest. In the French the evils of courtly chivalry are sensuality and homicide, and the virtues of 'celestial chivalry' are chastity and trust in God (as opposed to attachment to worldly things). Malory accepts the opposition between sensuality and chastity, but it is not of major importance for him. If we are to judge from his feelings about love, he probably found it difficult to understand why the French writer makes chastity the greatest of virtues (for Malory does not repudiate in his *Quest* all that he believes in elsewhere, whether of love or of chivalry). As for chivalry, Malory began without the presupposition of his source, that Lancelot's greatness as a knight was bound up with his love for Guinevere, and therefore he was not willing to condemn without qualification Lancelot's earlier life. He distinguished between right and wrong in chivalry, and began to see Lancelot's devotion to Guinevere simply as a betrayal of the right.

It has already been suggested that the French writer is not very interested in the life the Round Table knights ought to have led. Gawain, it is true, is told by a hermit that he was made a knight 'por ce que vos servissiez a nostre criator et deffendissiez Sainte Eglise . . .' (Pauphilet's text, p. 54). Malory altered this, in all probability, because he could find in it no real attempt to propose any kind of good secular life, or to draw upon the standards that the ideal of chivalry implied for him. He wrote:

> There [Gawain] tolde the eremyte how a monke of an abbay 'called me wycked knyght.'
>
> 'He myght well sey hit,' seyde the eremyte, 'for whan ye were first made knyght ye sholde have takyn you to knyghtly dedys and vertuous lyvyng. And ye have done the contrary, for ye have lyved myschevously many wyntirs' (*W* 891).

Professor Vinaver questions Malory's use of the phrase 'knightly deeds and virtuous living' to describe the 'duties of a good Christian', but Malory is not blind to the implications of the Quest on this level. There are repeated hints, fully borne out in the sequel, that one function of the Quest for him is to reconcile chivalry with Christian standards of conduct. To Malory there are two ways of life, that of the Quest, or perfection, and that of good chivalry. The standards of the second way are influenced by and in a sense derive from the religious discipline of the Quest, but that discipline is not in itself a way of life for all men—as it seemed to Malory that the French writer would make it. It is a renunciation of all attempt to live virtuously in secular life, a way that Malory will accept only when the life of chivalry has failed. The allegorical significance of the *Queste* has become obscured here, but there is no necessity to argue that Malory is trying to deprive the original of religious significance. He might have maintained, as the progress of Lancelot suggests both here and later, that the French writer has too narrow a view of the possible workings of grace.

However, beyond a certain point the Quest, as Malory relates it, is not subject to strictly logical procedure of interpretation (as the French is); the reader will lose rather than gain if he attempts to follow it through every remote and ambiguous passage. In defiance of the original, where nothing is left vague, many things must remain only of the vaguest import, for they belong to a realm of religious mystery for Malory. Such is the background of the story; what is central is the experience of Lancelot. He strives and falters as an ordinary man, labouring in a discipline that he does not completely understand, but knows to be good. His slightest reaction may be human:

> 'My synne and my wyckednes hath brought me unto grete dishonoure! . . .'
>
> So thus he sorowed tyll hit was day, and harde the fowlys synge: than somwhat he was comforted (*W* 896).

In the French version the sight of the sunshine and the sound of the birds serve only to increase Lancelot's misery. The contrast between Lancelot and Galahad again brings out the humanity of Malory's account of Lancelot. In the progress through this world of symbols and marvels, Galahad remains a figure-head, simply because he is created for that part. In Malory the strangeness of the Grail world remains, is even heightened, and Lancelot becomes a wanderer in it, abashed by his rare glimpses into mystery. If this was the result of Malory's lack of understanding, then his account is more significant than he realized. Lancelot's secular virtues, prowess and courtesy, assume new forms in the Quest, the one in his striving and the other in his attempt to put on humility. When in his glimpse of the Eucharist celebrated at Corbenic he is prompted to start forward and help the priest, courage and courtesy are fused in one characteristic gesture—'Fayre Fadir, Jesu Cryste, ne take hit for no synne if I helpe the good man whych hath grete nede of helpe' (*W* 1016). In spite of the warning, Lancelot goes into the chamber and is overwhelmed by the heavenly fire. More original and important is the presentation of Lancelot as a man who for all his strength and virtue lacks stability. 'Unstableness' is a rather vague and easily-invoked conception, but it is in a word the kind of weakness to which Lancelot gives way. He accepts penance, yet falls back into sin. The Quest may be read as a strange and difficult discipline designed to test the quality of a man's life, and the testing effect is to be observed most of all in Lancelot when the discipline is relaxed. Malory's version is neither incoherent nor a mere awkward rendering of the French. Ignoring the preoccupations of his source, he contrives to suggest how religious ideas interpenetrate the ideals of chivalry. These things are made meaningful through the experience of Lancelot, and in him their promise is great.

[IV]

At the beginning of the *Book of Sir Launcelot and Guinevere* Lancelot makes an attempt to fulfil the duties of a Christian knight, the defence of 'ladyes and damesels which dayly resorted unto hym that besoughte hym to be their champion', even though his motive is partly expediency. This, we may infer, is the way of 'knightly deeds and virtuous living', but Lancelot cannot live up to it. Guinevere banishes him for his lukewarmness, and this drives him to ever greater and more questionable exertions for the sake of her favour.

A number of episodes follow. They appear at first to be largely irrelevant and to illustrate only Malory's habit of remodelling the continuous French narrative into separate stories. But the sequence here—or rather, the mere appearance together—of these episodes is peculiar to Malory, and each has a definite relation to the main story: the overwhelming of Lancelot which follows his defection from the path of right conduct open to him.

The central event of this story is Lancelot's abduction of Guinevere; he rescues her and defends her regardless of the consequences, and this commitment can in the earlier episodes be seen growing in strength. In the episode of the poisoned apple it is comparatively innocent, for Guinevere is innocent, but it is noticeable that in defending her Lancelot shows no hesitation—nothing of the fear attributed to him in the French version 'de se desloiauter', of fighting in a wrongful cause. In the context of Malory's story the point of Guinevere's peril is that it offers Lancelot an opportunity of regaining her favour simply by his prowess. He saves her again when she is accused of adultery by Meleagant, but this time she is not innocent. Meleagant is killed at the behest of Guinevere, but not before he has touched Lancelot's conscience:

'My lorde sir Launcelot', seyde sir Mellyagaunce, 'I rede you beware what ye do; for thoughe ye ar never so good a knyght, as I wote well ye ar renowned the beste knyght of the worlde, yet shulde ye be avysed to do batayle in a wronge quarell, for God woll have a stroke in every batayle' (*W* 1133).

But Lancelot had promised the queen 'ever to be her knyght in ryght othir in wronge', as he tells Arthur after her rescue from Mador. The same unqualified 'in right or wrong' appears again when he has to fight his way out of her chamber. This was the fault that caused him humiliation in the Quest. Malory appears to be alluding to it again in his reflections on love and knighthood at the opening of *The Knight of the Cart* episode:

Therefore, lyke as May moneth flowryth and floryshyth in every mannes gardyne, so in lyke wyse lat every man of worshyp florysh hys herte in thys worlde: firste unto God, and nexte unto the joy of them that he promysed hys feythe unto; for there was never worshypfull man nor worshypfull woman but they loved one bettir than another; and worshyp in armys may never be foyled. But first reserve the honoure to God, and secundely thy quarell muste com of thy lady. And such love I calle vertuouse love (*W* 1119).

These remarks must surely be considered as relating to Lancelot and Guinevere: they are the noble man and woman who cannot help loving. The knight who is great in prowess would seem to be safe always in his love—his honour can never be trampled upon. But service of the lady must not be put first; if it is, the love is no longer virtuous. We may even recall Arthur's original charge to the Round Table knights: 'Also that no man take no batayles in a wrongeful quarell for no love . . .' (*W* 120), for the implications of both passages are the same.

With his first resort to arms against the Round Table it is apparent that Lancelot is blinded to questions of right and wrong by the struggle of the moment: he relies on his prowess alone. 'Jesu mercy ! he ys a mervaylous knyght of proues', Arthur says when he learns of Lancelot's escape from Agravain's trap. But when Gawain urges that Lancelot will be able in some way to prove his innocence, Arthur replies:

'That I beleve well . . . but I woll not that way worke with sir Launcelot, for he trystyth so much uppon hys hondis and hys myght that he doutyth no man' (*W* 1175; not in sources).

Lancelot's own speeches bear out this bitter comment. On four or five occasions he boasts that he can prove Guinevere's innocence by combat, and in referring to his escape from Agravain he adds, 'had nat the myght of God bene with me, I myght never have endured with [i.e. against] fourtene knyghts'. All this is expanded in Malory from two lines in the stanzaic *Morte Arthur*:

> 'Iffe any man sayes she is noght clene,
> I profre me there-fore to feght.' (ll. 2386–7).

In the same spirit Malory heightens the element of pride in Lancelot. In several long speeches Lancelot insists that he has been ill-rewarded by Arthur and Gawain, and boasts of his superiority to them in the field; and when he is banished—

'. . . in thys realme I had worshyp, and be me and myne all the hole Rounde Table hath bene encreced more in worshyp, by me and myne, than ever hit was by ony of you all' (*W* 1201).

It might seem that in insisting that he can prove Guinevere's innocence, and in his boastful self-justification. Lancelot is simply acting in the spirit of a long tradition of chivalric romance. Here Malory's version of the Tristram story offers a comparison. More than once when he is arraigned for his love of Isode, Tristram boasts of his prowess, and recalls his past achievements. But although Malory did not at heart believe in Tristram's self-justification or accept his adultery, he could not discover in himself or in his text any way of criticizing him—he was too obviously the hero and a knight of worship. There was at first a similar difficulty with Lancelot, but once he had discovered a standpoint from which he might criticize Lancelot, Malory could expose his fault in the story. Lancelot is to be judged by the code of knighthood which emerges throughout the *Morte Darthur*.

The aspect of this code which Malory emphasizes in the climax of the story is its regard for loyalty and fellowship among the Round Table knights. Consider the *Great*

Tournament of Book VII. This apparently irrelevant and trivial episode exemplifies the seriousness of Malory's regard for chivalry. But the illustration of loyalty is specially relevant at this juncture, for this is the last tournament of the Round Table knights before the great quarrel, and in it Arthur and his followers and Lancelot and his fight in friendly rivalry. Gareth, whose death at Lancelot's hands is the immediate cause of the war that follows, is singled out for his loyalty:

Also kynge Arthure blamed sir Gareth because he leffte hys felyshyp and hylde with sir Launcelot.

'My lorde,' seyde sir Garethe, 'he made me knyght, and whan I saw hym so hard bestad, methought hit was my worshyp to helpe hym . . . I shamed to se so many good knyghtes ayenste hym alone.'

'Now truly,' seyde kynge Arthur unto sir Gareth, 'ye say well, and worshypfully have ye done, and to youreselff grete worshyp . . .' (*W* 1114).

Arthur adds much more in the same vein; the incident is almost entirely Malory's invention, it seems, and the spirit of this dialogue is certainly his. As if to clinch the implicit comparison with later events he concludes: 'And he that was curteyse, trew, and faythefull to hys frynde was that tyme cherysshed.'

This is the fellowship that Lancelot betrays and destroys, and Malory makes many further adjustments in his narrative which stress that this tragedy matters far more than the discovery and end of Lancelot and Guinevere's love. It is noteworthy that in Malory's account Guinevere plays no active part in the story between her farewell to Lancelot in her chamber and her retreat to Amesbury. The cause of the quarrel is now pushed aside, an emphasis that recalls Malory's handling of the Tristram love-story. The presentation of Arthur is changed for the same end. Malory makes him put the discovery of adultery second, and emphasizes his affection for Lancelot. Instead of the jealous and furious outbursts of the French version we find many laments for the catastrophe that will now befall the Round Table:

'. . . Wyte you well, my harte was never so hevy as hit ys now. And much more I am soryar for my good knyghtes losse than for the losse of my fayre quene; for quenys I myght have inow, but such a felyship of good kynghtes shall never be togydirs in no company. And now I dare sey there was never Crystyn kynge that ever hylde such a felyshyp togydyrs . . .' (*W* 1183–4).

As a complementary process we see in Lancelot at first the growth of uneasiness at his own conduct, and then later complete consciousness of his error, followed by repentance. Malory contrives to suggest that the possibility of this self-realization is always present in Lancelot—it is only temporarily blinded during the fighting. The suggestion that he is uneasy about his devotion to Guinevere is obvious in the opening dialogue of Book VII, and it is accentuated by the manner in which Guinevere deals with him. After the tournament at Astolat, in which she thought Lancelot was false to her, she sent for him, 'and prayed hym of mercy, for why that she had ben wrothe wyth hym causeles'.

'Thys ys nat the first tyme,' seyde sir Launcelot . . . 'But, madame, ever I muste suffir you, but what sorow that I endure, ye take no forse.' (*W* 1098.)

Again in *The Knight of the Cart* she humiliates him, by spurning his zeal to defend her, and when he is taken aback she lightly asks, 'Do you forthynke youreselff of youre good dedis?' An impression is created that in each quarrel for Guinevere's sake Lancelot is less justified in his own eyes. At the same time, the episode of the Maid of Astolat casts doubt on the rightness of their love. Here, it will be remembered, Malory openly contrasts two kinds of love-relationship, marriage and love of paramours. There is no explicit reference to Lancelot's love for Guinevere, yet Malory's preference for a certain kind of love sets up an uneasy opposition within the story.

Once the great quarrel has begun, the uneasiness of Lancelot takes a more definite form. It appears at the outset in his doubts over rescuing Guinevere—'peradventure I shall there destroy som of my beste fryndis, and that shold moche repente me' (*W* 1172; not in source). Later, in battle, his followers twice urge him to put forth his full strength.

'Alas,' seyde sir Launcelot. 'I have no harte to fyght ayenste my lorde Arthur, for ever mesemyth I do nat as me ought to do' (*W* 1193).

In the verbal exchanges with Arthur and Gawain, Malory contrives to suggest how Lancelot is torn between his loyalty to his former companions, and his desire to sweep them from the field in proud confidence of his own superiority. This reflection of a struggle inside Lancelot is almost entirely Malory's invention; the English source merely gives hints for its development, and the French suggests that Lancelot (in spite of his desire to spare Arthur) looks on this war as little different from any other.

Lancelot's complete realization of his sin becomes apparent at the death of Guinevere, and at his own death. Guinevere, whose motives in Malory are sincerely religious, flies to a nunnery; and in her farewells to Lancelot there is no suggestion that the world of chivalry was well lost for love:

'. . . For as well as I have loved the heretofore, myne harte woll nat serve now to se the; for thorow the and me ys the floure of kyngis and knyghtes destroyed' (*W* 1252).

In the French version the lovers embrace and kiss on parting.[1] Malory makes Guinevere die beseeching God that she may never see Lancelot again, and when he goes to see her tomb Lancelot swoons over it, not for love, but because he remembers 'how by my defaute and myn orgule and my pryde that they were bothe layed ful lowe'. Nor does he die as Guinevere's lover. He has repented, and asks to be buried in Joyous Garde not because of its association with Guinevere but 'bycause of brekyng of myn avowe', i.e. merely in order not to break an oath. (The occasion on which the oath was made is not recorded.)

Malory's treatment of the religious part of the history confirms this interpretation of Lancelot's progress. Two acts in the story can be discerned, the first beginning with Lancelot's relapse after the Quest and ending with the episode called *The Healing of Sir Urry*, the second ending with Lancelot's death as a holy man. In the first, Lancelot's

[1] [v. pp. 108-10 below, where the version in the stanzaic *Morte Arthur* is also discussed.—Ed.]

uneasiness over his service of Guinevere is associated with Malory's adjuration, 'firste reserve the honoure to God'. Lancelot's healing of Urry carries the implication that in spite of his pride and his error, he retains the capacity for humility. He alone among Arthur's knights is able to heal the wounded knight, and the reason given is that he is the best knight in the world; but his behaviour recalls the qualification in the Quest that he is the best of earthly sinful men: he weeps 'as he had bene a chylde that had bene beatyn' (*W* 1152; the *sens* of the episode may be attributed to Malory).

The movement which leads, after the ensuing catastrophe, to Lancelot's complete repentance, begins not so much with his offer to Gawain to do penance for the knights killed around the stake as with the death of Gawain. Gawain has died confessing his wilfulness and pride, and beseeching Lancelot to visit his tomb. Later there follows Lancelot's visit and penance, an addition which Malory regards as important. But the decisive factor is the influence of Guinevere, whose end has already been mentioned. It is not for her sake that he renounces the world; it is rather that her renunciation leaves him free at last to make his. When she doubts the firmness of his resolution he can say that there is nothing now to move it, 'For in the queste of the Sankgreall I had that tyme forsakyn the vanytees of the worlde, had nat youre love bene'. Malory had, I think, always understood the Quest literally, as an injunction to enter the monastic life; and when, in returning to Guinevere, Lancelot 'forgate the promyse and the perfeccion that he made in the queste', he forgot both the promise he had made to lead a better life and the actual monastic discipline of the Quest, the way of perfection that inspired the promise. Lancelot now enters upon the way of perfection because, in the fall of the Round Table, secular life has broken down—the ideals of earthly chivalry have been superseded. Of the three predictions made about Lancelot in the Quest the last is now fulfilled:

'For I dare sey, as synfull as ever sir Launcelot hath byn, sith that he wente into the queste of the Sankgreal he slew never man nother nought shall, tylle that he com to Camelot agayne; for he hath takyn upon hym to forsake synne. And nere were that he ys nat stable, but by hys thoughte he ys lyckly to turne agayne, he sholde be nexte to encheve hit sauff sir Galahad, hys sonne; but God knowith hys thought and hys unstablenesse. And yett shall he dye ryght an holy man, and no doute he hath no felow of none erthly synfull man lyvyng' (*W* 948; not in source).

[V]

The extent of Malory's originality and achievement in the culmination of his book needs to be stressed. Professor Vinaver has shown how skilfully he develops the conflict of personal loyalties, but this is only part of the machinery of the final action. What gives this account of the conflict unusual force is the fact that it takes place in a world of value and judgement. 'Nullus strenuus miles nisi amat: amor facit strenuitatem militiae': in rejecting this ideal for what he believes to be a better one Malory gives the story a moral and finally justifies the seriousness with which he regards chivalry.

The originality becomes apparent if we contrast the frame of events in the *Morte Darthur* with that of the French cycle. In the latter the *Queste* is followed, as in Malory, by the *Morte Artu*, but there is no vital connexion between the two sections. The *Queste* appears not to envisage a sequel, for it makes no predictions about the fall of the Round Table as it actually happens, and admits no hint that its judgements are not final. The author of the *Mort Artu*, on the other hand, makes no effort to suggest continuity, and there is a touch of worldliness in the religious references in his story, especially in the conclusion. ('La platitude de ce dénouement,' Albert Pauphilet wrote, 'ne fait qu'accentuer la différence d'esprit de ce livre avec la *Queste*.')[1] The supernatural element and binding force in this part of the cycle is simply Fate, a pagan conception barely tinged with Christianity. The two narratives are set in different worlds, and to accept, as some critics would, the vague belief of the compilers of the cycle, that the Round Table was destroyed because it had offended God, is to gloss over the disparity between them.

[1] *Le Legs du Moyen Age*, p. 217.

Here, where the French is weak, Malory is strong. He binds the *Quest* and the *Morte Arthur* together through the development of Lancelot's character, and in the later conflict so develops the sense of personal choice in his characters that the conception of Fate becomes almost superfluous. In the culminating blow against the Round Table Mordred is not the instrument of destiny (or another victim of the *force d'amours*), but a traitor whose rebellion is the final instance of the failure of loyalties. The weakness of the *Mort Artu* is that its author has no certain standard by which to assess and judge the conflicting ideals of love and chivalry; for him, indeed, the two aspects were scarcely to be distinguished. By contrast, the author of the *Queste* brought to courtly romance a religious test, and it is plain that he judged and condemned. For Pauphilet this is his peculiar achievement. In his *Études sur la Queste del Saint Graal* he remarks upon the incomplete satisfaction of reading in the *matière de Bretagne* because of its endless fantasy without purpose. The great merit of the author of the *Queste*, he suggests, is that he gives a point to romance material and satisfies the intellect as well as the imagination. It is true that the French author achieves this end; he achieves it through a moral purpose, and his conclusions are in part comparable with Malory's. For in Malory's story of Lancelot unvirtuous love is ultimately rejected, and the worldly fiction of courtly romance is superseded by religious values. But there is a difference in manner. In the process of giving significance to the Grail romance the French author almost completely destroys the original life of the material and its persons. There is a judgement on love and chivalry, but it does not emerge of its own accord; fantasy is manœuvred to yield a moral, and *sens* and *matière* are disjunctive. In Malory's story of the fall of Lancelot, on the other hand, love and chivalry are both presented sympathetically, and the reader has no feeling that the moral is ready-made, or that he is told what to approve. The narrative makes its own point, and *sens* and *matière* are one. In the content and in its method this story may be compared with two other English medieval stories about chivalry. In the *Knight's Tale* the conventions appear to be used simply as material for a story, yet in his own way Chaucer reveals the inherent values of the action; in the death of Arcite and in the speech of Theseus he suggests that the outer forms of chivalry may conceal an ideal that can make for noble conduct. In *Sir Gawain and the Green Knight* the parallel is even closer, because there the formal virtues of chivalry are strongly emphasized. Again the writer is not simply telling a story; he shows that courtesy does not reside in good manners alone, nor even in keeping a promise, important though these things are; it is a moral virtue, implying once again nobility of conduct. Like Malory, too, the Gawain poet takes it for an established truth that conduct of this kind is essentially Christian. In all three works the material of romance becomes the vehicle of a serious purpose, and yet the moral is expressed through the story, and arises naturally. Hence to understand Malory's presentation of Lancelot is to grasp the unity of his book: its theme is loyalty, and the story of Lancelot gives a high place to loyalty even in describing its failure.

Malory was able to discover a new meaning in this story because from the beginning chivalry had a value for him outside romance, but we should not conclude that his belief in chivalry was particularly practical. Both Malory and Caxton (whose praise of the book's moral worth is still the best) wrote at a time when moral literature was understood to have definite practical implications—a view which survives in the Preface to the *Faerie Queene*. Thus in Caxton's remarks on the *Morte Darthur* it seems legitimate to distinguish between what is contemporary and practical and what is ideal. In the first he speaks for his time, when chivalric practice (such as it ever was) was not remote, even if outmoded; in the second he speaks for later ages, though still in his own terms. In the book itself the practical and topical aspects are completely subordinate to the purpose of the story. Even the appeal to Englishmen ('se ye nat what a myschyff here was?'), though of contemporary interest, is far more important for its place in the context. The moral of the story is given added force by being generalized: all earthly loyalty is at an end when that which held the Round Table together has failed in its own knights. Chivalric romance is a literary convention. It would not exist, or at least would not seem so significant to us, if chivalry had not once been an institution, and Malory's preference for a certain kind of loyalty is historical in the wider sense, that it is closer to practical, martial chivalry than is the courtly fiction of his French sources. But even this chivalry is idealized in the *Morte Darthur*. What we see is the portrayal of a kind of excellence, and it is this that Hector epitomizes in his threnody over the corpse of Lancelot (*W* 1259). The connexions between courtesy and bearing a shield, between fidelity and bestriding a horse, seem irrelevant and illogical unless we realize that for Malory chivalry was the outward and temporal expression of inner and timeless virtues.

6

Lancelot's Penance

F. WHITEHEAD

ALTHOUGH the French *Mort Artu* begins with an ominous reference[1] to the infatuation of Lancelot, who has been back from the Grail quest only one month when he renews his liaison with Guinevere, the expectation that, as in the *Queste del Saint Graal*, the theme of Lancelot's sinful life will be given special prominence in the story is not borne out by subsequent events. So far from condemning Lancelot, the *Mort Artu* extols him. In its treatment of the adultery motif, it is a close, and in some respects a servile, imitation of the *Tristan* legend[2] and displays the same highly ambiguous, not to say hypocritical, attitude towards the moral issues.

As in the *Tristan*, the lovers are betrayed[3] to Arthur by a traitor, Agravain, whose action is condemned by his own brothers; it is Agravain who advises[4] that the queen be put to death; Gawain, when[5] he hears of the proposal, renounces his allegiance to Arthur, and Gareth, who is subsequently to be slain by Lancelot, consents only under compulsion to guard the queen, and announces his intention of avoiding battle with Lancelot if the latter comes to rescue her.[6] After

[1] *La Mort le Roi Artu*, ed. J. Frappier (Paris, 1936), 5, 9–15. All references to the *Mort Artu* are to the page and line numbers of this edition.

[2] *Mort Artu* 85, 17–102, 23 (the discovery of the lovers, the attempt to capture them, their flight to Joyous Garde) corresponds roughly to Béroul 573–1278, while *Mort Artu* 129, 1–136, 11, are a very free imitation of some features of Béroul 2350–926. The *point de départ* for the scene of the murder of Gareth is probably the account in the prose *Tristan* of the slaying of one of Andret's companions by Tristan during his escape from the king's justice (B.N. français 103, fol. 76 r/a: for the text, see Bédier, *Le Roman de Tristan par Thomas*, II (Paris, 1905), p. 358).

[3] Ibid. 85, 26–95, 18. [4] 96, 15–97, 3.

[5] 97, 4–14. [6] 98, 11–19.

the killing of Gareth and his brothers and the flight of Lancelot and Guinevere to Joyous Garde, Arthur and Gawain take up arms against the hero.[1] Lancelot, who does not wish to fight the king, not because he fears him but because he loves him,[2] sends a messenger to inquire why Arthur is in the field:[3] there has been nothing wrong between himself and Guinevere, and he is ready to prove this by judicial combat to the satisfaction of a court.[4] As regards Arthur's nephews, his conscience is clear,[5] since they brought about their own deaths. The dispute between Arthur and Lancelot over Guinevere is eventually settled when Lancelot's willingness to surrender Guinevere and go into exile convinces Arthur that they cannot be guilty lovers.[6] The feud over the slaughter of Arthur's nephews goes on, owing to Gawain's thirst for vengeance; it ends only with the single combat between Lancelot and Gawain,[7] in which Gawain is worsted. The result is a story in which the conduct of Lancelot is justified not only in his own eyes but in those of the author. He is represented as a chivalrous gentleman who is under a duty to defend the queen's life and honour and who, in the course of his duty, slays, unwittingly and unwillingly, a friend who at heart warmly sympathizes with his championship of Guinevere. In the difficult situation which results, he behaves in every respect as a chivalrous knight should: concerned more to protect Guinevere's good name than to indulge his passion;[8] regardful of his knightly dignity, which will not allow him to sacrifice his honour, i.e. his standing in the eyes of his fellows,[9] but at the same time most reluctant to carry on the war if there is an honourable chance of ending it;[10] willing to make the most ample reparation for the death of Gareth and even to abase himself before Gawain if this will persuade the latter to drop the feud.[11] It is Gawain's obstinacy that leads to the single combat in which he fails to

[1] 111, 22–112, 5. [2] 115, 27–30. [3] 115, 32–116, 2.
[4] 116, 2–7. [5] 116, 7–11. [6] 131, 20–22, 133, 21–23.
[7] 170, 4–177, 15.
[8] This is the reason why he agrees to surrender Guinevere to Arthur: 130, 12–18.
[9] 161, 8–17. [10] 163, 22–166, 1. [11] 166, 2–20.

prove Lancelot guilty of treason[1] and in which Lancelot refuses to take his enemy's life,[2] just as he has previously not merely refused to lay hands on Arthur's person but intervened to save him after he has been unhorsed by Hector.[3] If Lancelot is absent from the last great battle with Mordred, this is due to the king's reluctance to send for him,[4] although he has been warned by a supernatural vision[5] that only with the aid of Lancelot can he avert defeat. As soon as he hears that Arthur is dead and the queen in peril, he crosses over to Logres,[6] but finds that the queen has died[7] in the cloister in which she had taken refuge, and avenges her death and the king's on the sons of Mordred.[8]

Nothing in the concluding section of the work—in which Lancelot retires into a hermitage—mars the splendour of his chivalry. Rich in earthly renown, but with his lord and lady dead and the fellowship to which he belonged destroyed, and finding that the archbishop of Canterbury and his cousin Blioberis have entered religion, he decides that, having shared with them the delights of this world, he will bear them company in the life they have now chosen.[9] The emphasis in this last chapter is not on the sins for which Lancelot is now doing penance, but on the exemplary piety of his new life and his attachment to spiritual exercises.[10] To earthly fame there is now added heavenly felicity. The epitaph in Joyous Garde[11] give us the final verdict: 'Ci gist li cors Galeholt, le segnor des Lointaignes Illes, et avec lui repose Lancelos del Lac, qui fu li mieudres chevaliers qui onques entrast el roiaume de Logres, fors seulement Galaad son fill.' Hector's great eulogy of Lancelot in Malory,[12] although marked by a passionate intensity of emotion completely foreign to the *Mort Artu*, is nevertheless in complete accordance with the French author's attitude.

If some critics are inclined to stress the fact that Lancelot

[1] 176, 12–177, 1. [2] 177, 17–21. [3] 127, 17–128, 4.
[4] 201, 16–202, 6. [5] 199, 26–200, 5. [6] 228, 1–24.
[7] 229, 23–29. [8] 229, 29–231, 30. [9] 233, 1–234, 5.
[10] 235, 7–10: et li arcevesques l'avoit ja tant mené que Lancelos avoit ordre de prouvoire, si qu'il chantoit chascun jour messe et qu'il estoit de si grant abstinence qu'il ne menjoit fors pain et eve et racines qu'il cueilloit en la broce.
[11] 237, 22–25. [12] *W* 1259.9–21.

is a sinful man, rather than the 'best of all sinful men', which is obviously how Malory and the author of the *Mort Artu* want to regard him, the reason is doubtless that it is difficult for the modern mind to idealize a hero who combines feudal devotion to an overlord with a romantic attachment to the lady who happens to be that overlord's wife. A Lancelot fighting against a deeply loved overlord is a tolerable figure as long as the contention is about Gareth, whom Lancelot has slain by mischance and whose death Arthur feels bound to avenge. A Lancelot who loves Arthur much and Guinevere more is a somewhat dubious character. Nevertheless, it seems that we are meant to admire him in both of these incompatible roles.[1]

The difficulties of the story are mitigated by allowing the Lancelot-Guinevere story to recede into the background well before the end, the interest being concentrated instead on Gawain's feud with Lancelot and then on Mordred's rebellion. Guinevere's behaviour during the rebellion is that of a completely loyal wife: she resists when the barons try to force her to marry Mordred, even though a report has been set on foot that Arthur is dead; she garrisons the Tower of London and tries to hold out there, and finally takes refuge in a nunnery when it seems that Mordred will capture her.[2] Her pious death in the nunnery[3] is an epilogue to this last and completely worthy episode in her career.

The decision to end the *Mort Artu* without allowing Guinevere and Lancelot to meet again is surely the right one. The morrow of a disastrous defeat, when the Arthurian world has been destroyed beyond the hope of restoration and the survivors have no other course than to seek refuge in the cloister, is no time for new romantic entanglements. In

[1] The paradox comes out most strikingly in the scene (86, 22–87, 22) where Agravain and Mordred denounce Lancelot to the king. Agravain hates Lancelot, and Mordred is a villain of the deepest dye, while Gawain and Gareth are courteous knights who sympathize with Lancelot. But it is the bad characters who behave loyally towards Arthur (and unctuously remind him of the fact), whereas it is the good ones who are remiss in their feudal duty. However interested Agravain's motives, it is hard to disagree with his judgement on Lancelot: 'il vos est si loiaus qu'il vos fet desenneur de la reïne vostre fame et qu'il l'a conneüe charnelment'.

[2] 148, 14–157, 1; 190, 7–193, 4. [3] 229, 23–29.

the original *Mort Artu*, Guinevere dies as the 'good' queen who has taken the veil after her husband's death, and Lancelot as the 'good' knight who would have saved Logres if he had not been prevented.

The final meeting between Lancelot and Guinevere comes into the story as the result of an interpolation in a late redaction[1] now represented by MS. Palatinus Latinus 1967. This is an obvious *scène à faire* and it is not surprising that some *remanieur* was injudicious enough to attempt it. The starting-point is obviously the passage in the *Mort Artu* where Guinevere agrees with the nuns that if Arthur is victorious she shall rejoin him, but that if he is killed she shall take the veil.[2] After defeating the sons of Mordred, Lancelot comes by chance to the nunnery; the lovers are deeply moved by this encounter, and Lancelot is overcome by pity at seeing Guinevere in a nun's habit. He tells her that she can now be queen of the country if she wishes; she replies that she has already enjoyed all possible worldly honour; she reminds Lancelot that they have done 'what they should not have done' and that it is time that they devoted the remnant of their lives to the service of God. Lancelot is easily persuaded, and after a tender leave-taking, in which he asks her pardon for any wrongs he may have done her, rides away and arrives at the hermitage where he finds the Archbishop of Canterbury and Blioberis.

While the emotional encounter of Lancelot and Guinevere is a first step towards the reintroduction of the romantic theme, there is no suggestion in the Palatinus of any renewal of the love relationship; Lancelot merely invites Guinevere to take over the country, and her refusal of the offer is in accordance with her new-found reputation for piety. But a more pious Guinevere means a more worldly Lancelot, who simply follows the suggestions of the lady.

The stanzaic *Morte Arthur*[3] is derived from a version of

[1] Edited by J. Frappier as an appendix to his edition of the *Mort Artu* (pp. 239–40); v. also Frappier's article 'Sur un remaniement de la *Mort Artu*, *Romania* LVII (1931), pp. 214–22.

[2] 192, 18–193, 5.

[3] *Le Morte Arthur*, ed. J. D. Bruce (E.E.T.S. 1903). The references to the *Morte Arthur* are to the lines of this edition.

the *Mort Artu* that included the Palatinus interpolation.[1] In the *Morte Arthur* account, the theme of penance for former sin, treated in a dry and perfunctory way and along well-worn conventional lines in the *Mort Artu*, is infused with a passionate intensity of feeling only possible in a lyric poem. Guinevere is no longer content to remind Lancelot that he and she have done what they should not have done, but in the intensity of her self-reproach launches the accusation:

3638 Abbes, to you I knowlache here
  That throw thys ylke man And me,
For we togedyr han loved vs dere,
  All thys sorowfull werre hath be:
my lord is slayne, that had no pere,
  And many A doughty knyght and free:
Therefore for sorowe I dyed nere,
  As sone as I euyr hym gan see—

Whan I hym see, the sothe to say,
  All my herte bygan to colde,
That euyr I shuld abyde thys day,
  To see so many barons bolde
Shuld for vs be slayne away.

Her emotion on seeing Lancelot has nothing worldly about it; there is no remembrance of former affection breaking in on the present desolation, she is simply moved by the thought of the harm that she and Lancelot have wrought. This introduces the expression of her pious intention:

3654 Isette I am In suche a place,
  my sowle hele I wyll abyde,
Telle god send me som grace,
  Throw mercy of hys woundys wyde
That I may do so in thys place
  my synnys to amende thys ilke tyde,
After to haue a syght of hys face,
  At domys day on hys ryght syde.

Then follows the exhortation to Lancelot to forsake her company for ever and return to his own kingdom and take a wife. Lancelot refuses to 'work so great an unright against

[1] This occupies ll. 3606–745.

her';[1] since they have lived together for so long, he will continue to share her lot and retire, as she has done, into the cloister. Guinevere doubts the sincerity of his resolution, but he affirms that:

> 3702 As we in lykynge lyffed in fere,
> By mary moder, made and wyffe,
> Tyll god vs departe with dethes dere,
> To penance I yeld me here As blythe.

Then comes the sorrow of the lovers at their parting. Lancelot demands a kiss, but Guinevere, perhaps a little too smugly, reminds him that 'To absteyne vs we must haue thought'[2] and bids him think on his Redeemer and how in this world 'there is noght/But warre And stryffe And bataylle sore'.[3]

Starting with the motif of a pious Guinevere who persuades Lancelot to share her penance, the *Morte Arthur* has succeeded in giving quite a new colour to the story. It is her own guilt that distresses Guinevere, and she speaks rather as though it is the natural thing for knights to yield to their sensual instincts and for ladies to be under a special responsibility to safeguard their chastity. All she suggests therefore is that Lancelot should return to his own land, there to become a good king and a respectable husband. Lancelot feels that his first duty is to Guinevere, and he recoils from anything that looks like infidelity towards her. His resolution to retire from the world is therefore an act of self-identification with his lady. The scene is thus already what it is in Malory: an interview between a highly devout lady and a lover who has by no means forgotten his former romantic attachment.

The account in the *Morte Arthur* was taken over by Malory.[4] Few passages in Malory are more celebrated than his account of the last meeting, but we must not allow the immediacy of the scene and the stately cadences of the prose to disguise the fact that the handling of the psychological and religious issues is somewhat heavy-handed. The opening of the scene is far more delicately treated in the *Morte Arthur*: Guinevere swoons at the sight of Lancelot and has to be led to her

[1] 3683. [2] 3716. [3] 3720–1. [4] 1251, 28–1253, 33.

chamber; it is the abbess who brings Lancelot into her presence, and the explanation of her emotion—she has loved Lancelot, and with disastrous consequences—is made to the abbess privately.[1] In Malory, Guinevere is attended in the cloister by her 'ladyes and gentilwomen'; she has Lancelot brought before her and then denounces their joint sin to 'all tho ladys'. The discretion of the poetic text, in which she announces that she will abide here until:

> . . . god send me som grace,
> Throw mercy of hys woundys wyde. . . .

is destroyed by a paraphrase which shifts the emphasis so as to make the timid hope of divine mercy into a confident expectation of a heavenly reward.[2] Except for the fact that Malory's compressed and robust style makes Guinevere less exhortatory and more imperious, the rest of the scene follows the poem accurately down to the point where Guinevere expresses scepticism as to the sincerity of Lancelot's resolution to retire from the world. This gives Malory the opportunity to develop the theme of Lancelot's fidelity: he has in all things kept faith with Guinevere—because of her love, he refused to forsake the vanities of the world at the time of the Quest of the Grail; if he had done so, he would have done better in the quest than any knight save his son Galahad. One cannot read this as a reproach: it is not that Guinevere has thwarted his aspirations towards spirituality but that he has willingly sacrificed his renown on her behalf, counting this world (and the next) well lost for love. Now that Guinevere has entered on the road to perfection there is no reason why he should not do likewise and every reason why he should. That neither his soul's

[1] 3637: In covnselle there than sayd she thus.

[2] *W* 1252, 13: 'And yet I truste, thorow Goddis grace and thorow Hys Passion of Hys woundis wyde, that aftir my deth, I may have a syght of the blyssed face of Cryste Jesu, and on Doomesday to sytte on Hys ryght syde; for as synfull as ever I was, now ar seyntes in hevyn'. What is missing in Malory is any reference to penance on earth; moreover, the reference to the Redemption is made into a mere adverbial subjunct and thus subordinated to the idea of Guinevere's exaltation on the Judgement Day. What however makes the passage particularly disconcerting is the brazen assurance of Malory's own addition: 'for as synfull as ever I was, now ar seyntes in hevyn'.

health, nor the vanities of the world, nor anything else except the service of his lady matters can be seen from Malory's strange addition: 'For I take recorde of God, in you I have had myn erthly joye, and yf I had founden you now so dysposed, I had caste me to have had you into myn owne royame.'[1] The calling on the name of God, mere *façon de parler* though it be, is in the circumstances of the case somewhat incongruous. Moreover, the two French versions of the *Mort Artu* carefully avoid any suggestion that Arthur's death has left Lancelot a clear field; indeed, no courtly work in French allows the lovers to build on the prospect of the husband's death: there is too much bad conscience about adultery for that to be possible. Given the ambiguous relationship between Arthur and Lancelot, given the fact that the former was not merely Lancelot's rival in love but his most kind lord, the proposal seems more than a little indecent. That it is very cynical in this context, where it follows immediately Lancelot's declaration that he 'must needs take him to perfection', is obvious enough. His request for a kiss (*W* 1253, 26) is taken almost word for word from the *Morte Arthur*:[2] in Malory's new romantic setting it contributes further to the strangely profane impression that the passage makes.

To treat Malory's *Tale of the Death of King Arthur* as though it were an improving religious work, as though it discussed courtly morality in the light of the doctrine of the Grail, or even as though it showed the world and its vain joys dissolving into nothingness is, as Professor Vinaver has shown,[3] to place the emphasis where Malory has resolutely refused to put it. The general theme of thwarted affection and lament for former friends that fills the concluding chapters of Malory's work shapes our reaction to the passage in which, in an effusive lament over the bodies of Guinevere and of Arthur, Lancelot indulges in bitter self-reproach, and asserts that 'by my defaute and myn

[1] *W* 1253, 19–22.

[2] The *Morte Arthur* account is obviously an elaboration of Palatinus Latinus 1967 (p. 240, 19–21): Et Lancelos li prie qu'ele li pardoint tous mesfaiz, et ele dist que si fet ele mout volantiers, si le bese et acole u departir.

[3] *W* 1607–8; *The Tale of the Death of King Arthur*, pp. xxii–xxiii.

orgule and my pryde . . . they were bothe layed ful lowe that were pereles that ever was lyvynge of Cristen people'.[1] The lament, and the inordinate emotion that he displays from this time onwards: the broken slumbers, the refusal to be comforted, the grovelling on the queen's tomb, are not in keeping with the monastic way of life he has adopted, and represent the introduction into the calm of the cloister of those worldly affections he is supposed to have renounced. The *Mort Artu* has a religious message, albeit a trite one: in a world of mutability, where prosperity, happiness, and human life itself are mere incidents in the downward rush of things, there is no trust to trust in, save in penance for past sin and mortifications that may open the gates of Heaven. Malory perverts the message, by allowing two things to remain while all else changes: the power of human affection and the remembrance of the past.

[1] *W* 1256, 33–35.

7

Caxton and Malory

SALLY SHAW

A COMPARISON of the Winchester manuscript with Caxton's printed text of the *Morte Darthur* might raise hopes of finding striking differences between versions: differences easily classifiable, which might prove one text or other more faithful to a lost original, or fuller, or older, or demonstrably regional in its language. Careful study of the versions dashes these hopes. There are indeed differences, but apart from the treatment of Book V, few are striking, and conclusions must be drawn warily.

The two texts do not seem to be immediately related: it is probable that they descend, as it were, in cousinly fashion from two separate predecessors. But from two points of difference it seems likely that in spite of numerous blemishes the Winchester text represents the closer approximation to what Malory actually wrote. The first point is the very much fuller version of Book V found in Winchester: it seems almost certain that Caxton's text of this book represents his own deliberate re-writing. The other point is the presence throughout the rest of the Caxton version of traces of an editorial hand, ranging from the provision of new book and chapter divisions to the glossing of an unfamiliar word.

These signs of Caxton's editorial work, both in the work in general and in Book V in particular, are of considerable interest, and I hope to indicate them clearly enough for a reader to see what he is likely to gain or lose by choosing one version rather than the other. Today the scales are somewhat unfairly weighted against Caxton by the attractive presentation given to the Winchester manuscript in Professor Vinaver's edition. Should the reader be able, however, to go back to this manuscript itself, unpunctuated, unparagraphed, unchaptered, with no conveniently appended comparative readings to fill lacunae, his impressions might be different: and it is against this unedited manuscript that I shall judge Caxton's print.

Since it seems for various reasons unlikely that Caxton's exemplar was identical with the Winchester text, it cannot be definitely proved that Caxton was responsible for every variant reading found in his version, nor is this indeed probable. Some of these variants are certainly mere scribal slips. Yet a great many other variants remain which seem exceedingly likely to stem from Caxton's editorial conscience. That he took his editorial responsibilities seriously is clear from his famous Preface to the *Morte Darthur*: but neither from this nor from his other Prefaces can one deduce just how far he considered an editor's privilege should extend over his text. In the Malory Preface he says: 'And I accordyng to my copye haue doon sette it in enprynte': but the internal evidence of Book V suggests very strongly that he took it upon himself to alter and abridge that copy where he thought it necessary. Some interesting passages in his Prohemye and Epilogues to the *Polycronicon* (1482) bear out this suspicion: 'sette in forme by me William Caxton', he writes, 'and a lytel embelyshed fro tholde makyng'; and again, 'and somwhat have chaunged the rude and old Englyssh/that is to wete certayn wordes/which in these dayes be neither vsyd ne vnderstanden'.

Apart from the special case of Book V, the most obvious difference between Caxton's print and the Winchester MS. is in the presentation of the text. Although Caxton was not responsible for the order in which the tales appear, credit must be given to him for the semblance of continuity and order which regular book and chapter divisions have brought to his text.

His influence seems plain in the alterations found in his version of the colophons, or concluding words, of some of Malory's tales. He has by his own admission redivided certain of these tales, making a total of twenty-one books instead of Winchester's eight: these twenty-one he has chaptered, and has provided with appropriate rubrics in a table of contents; and he has added pointing.

Signs of editing are clear and interesting in the Caxton colophons. An example is the one which concludes Malory's *Tale of King Arthur*; it is the first found in the MS. and in Caxton is at the end of Book IV. In Winchester it runs:

Here endyth this tale, as the Freynshe booke seyth, from the maryage of kynge Uther unto kynge Arthure that regned aftir hym and ded many batayles. And this booke endyth whereas sir Launcelot and sir Trystrams com to courte. Who that woll make ony more lette hym seke other bookis of kynge Arthure or of sir Launcelot or sir Trystrams: for this was drawyn by a knyght presoner, sir Thomas Malleorré, that God sende hym good recover. Amen. Explicit (*W* 180).

All this is omitted by Caxton, who substitutes merely 'Explicit liber quartus'. His reasons seem clear. First, the personal references are out of place in the middle of the book (a similar passage at the very end appears fully in Caxton). Secondly, the implication that there is no more to follow is nonsense when seventeen more books are still ahead. Finally, even if Caxton had left out the personal element and the advice to those 'that woll make ony more', there would still have been the recapitulation to make a more decided break between Books IV and V than he would have wished. He seems to have aimed at equally emphasized book divisions throughout, so that the narrative should never be brought up short.

The treatment of this colophon is typical. In the seven succeeding colophons there are five references to the author in the Winchester versions and all except the final one are omitted by Caxton. This last one is not in Winchester (the final gathering being missing), but Caxton's text has:

Here is the ende of the hoole book of kyng Arthur & of his noble knyghtes of the rounde table/that when they were hole togyders there was euer an C and XL/and here is the ende of the deth of Arthur/I praye you all Ientyl men and Ientyl wymmen that redeth this book of Arthur and his knyghtes from the begynnyng to the endying/praye for me whyle I am on lyue that god sende me good delyueraunce/& whan I am deed I praye you all praye for my soule/for this book was ended the ix yere of the reygne of kyng edward the fourth/by syr Thomas Maleore knyght/as Ihesu helpe hym for hys grete myght/as he is the seruaunt of Ihesu bothe day and nyght/.

Caxton then adds his own colophon to the whole volume.

The colophon cited is unlike the others in Caxton. Its reference to the author and his situation, and its appeal for intercession both to God and to the readers, correspond closely to other colophon readings found in the MS., and it probably also corresponds to what Malory actually wrote. At the end of his whole volume Caxton would feel mention of the author's name and circumstances to be appropriate, and a prayer almost a necessity.

Caxton was also faced with the problem of suitably subdividing his material, for the divisions as indicated by the Winchester colophons made up books of very unequal length. The Tales of *King Arthur*, the *Sankgreal* and especially *Tristram* were many times longer than *Arthur and Lucius* (even in its unabridged form) or *Gareth*. In his Preface he takes responsibility for this: 'And for to vnderstonde bryefly the contente of thys volume/I haue deuyded it in to xxi bookes/and euery book chapytred as here after shal by goddes grace folowe/'. His aim seems to have been to make books of roughly equal length, each containing as far as possible a single main theme. Some of his material proved intractable, but on the whole his book division can be justified either by the text or on grounds of sheer necessity.

The dividing places sometimes present themselves obviously. The story of Balin and Balan, for example, is of a suitable length for a book, and can be easily detached from surrounding material. On other occasions it is easy to begin a new book, not so easy to end it: the story of Sir La Cote Male Tayle in the *Tristram* section illustrates this hazard. This Book (IX) actually ends in the middle of a conversation between King Arthur and Sir Tristram. Caxton, presumably in desperation, seizes on a reference, itself the result of a previous scribal misunderstanding, to a 'first and second book of Tristram', as an excuse for a much-needed break.

Once out of the *Tristram* wilderness, Caxton found the *Sankgreal* book also inconveniently long, but only too well signposted, and the result is six very short books. The divisions are on the whole sensible; but the whole Grail episode is actually shorter in number of chapters than

Caxton's Book X, and it is open to question whether it would not have been better left undivided.

It must be admitted that the break at Caxton's Book XVIII seems ill-placed. The reflective digression on love and spring is placed at the end of Book XVIII, while Guinevere's unlucky Maying expedition, which surely inspired it, is held over to begin Book XIX. A break at about this point, where an entirely new episode begins, is certainly wanted: but the only conceivable reason for Caxton's separating this 'prologue' from the incident to which it refers could be the wish to gain continuity by giving the reader a hint of what is to come.

There was no formula in the text to encourage Caxton to make the division between Books XX and XXI. His sense of the dramatic and fitting must have guided him to make a separate book for the final tragedy. Arthur is besieging Lancelot's French castle when 'ryght so cam tydyngis unto kynge Arthur frome Inglonde that made kynge Arthur and all hys oste to remeve'. Caxton's version is identical with this Winchester reading, but he adds, 'Here foloweth the xxi book'. The change of scene from France to England makes an appropriate place for the break.

On the whole Caxton does his work of subdivision well. Book X remains disproportionately long and Book XV as disproportionately short: yet by pruning phrases, he has succeeded in making the original book divisions, with their colophons, less final, and he has sometimes emphasized his own new divisions by adding words or phrases to existing formulas. The result is that the pauses between books seem to have equal value, and the work is no longer the eight separate romances found in the Winchester MS., but one volume whose component books, partly self-contained but usually too short to stand alone, form one coherent whole.

In the same way that it has been divided into books, Caxton's print is further subdivided into 507 chapters. Rubrics are provided for each in a table of contents; usually Caxton prefers to mention one incident only in each rubric, which makes for easy reading but means that important details are sometimes omitted, especially where action continues through more than one chapter.

It is quite reasonable to assume that this chaptering was, as he himself implied, largely Caxton's own work. In the Winchester MS. there are no comparable divisions; there are, however, red initials, sometimes preceded by a blank leaf or a space, or followed by a phrase in large red letters, which occur throughout the MS. at irregular intervals. Of these 106 initials 104 correspond to a new chapter in Caxton (the other two occur in much abridged passages of the Arthur and Lucius episode). This suggests that in this respect Caxton's copy resembled Winchester, and that for these chapters at least he was merely following it.

Apart from those which mark an obvious pause in the story, most of these initials appear where some action begins, or at the beginning or end of direct speech. Many apparently suitable dividing places are not marked at all, and often when they do occur these red letters seem to denote emphasis as much as a pause in the narrative.

We cannot tell whether Caxton's copy had exactly the same number of red initials as in the MS.; it may well have had more. Whether or not this copy helped his work in this respect, the text itself in very many instances made his work easy. Such phrases as 'so leve we' or 'now turneth the tale' abound and clearly mark a change of subject. A typical example is at the beginning of Chapter 82 of Book X, which runs:[1] 'Now leve we of this mater and speke we of sir Palomides that rode and lodged with the two kynges all that nyght.' Some other formulas occurring at chapter divisions are 'This meanwhyle', 'Then felle new tydyngys', 'So lette we this passe and turne we'. Episodes like the short and self-contained quests of certain knights like Torre, Pellinore, and Gawain provide convenient chapters, as do the separate days of the great tournaments. Sometimes formulas occur very close together, and this occasionally results in a very short chapter, though usually Caxton will ignore them in such cases.

Many chapters begin, failing a completely new subject or episode, with arrivals, meetings, partings, or with the commencement of a new minor incident. A conversation or speech, especially when immediately followed by action,

[1] Winchester is quoted unless the contrary is indicated.

often starts a new chapter. Occasionally a break comes in the middle of a long conversation if there is a noticeable change in subject or tone: for example, in Book XIII, Chapters 2/3, this passage occurs, the new chapter coming at the point where Arthur, having failed with Lancelot, tries to get Gawain to draw the magic Grail sword:

Than sir Launcelot answerde full sobirly, 'Sir, that ys nat my swerde: also I have no hardines to sette my honde thereto, for hit longith nat to hange be my syde. Also, who that assayth to take hit and faylith of that swerde, he shall resseyve a wounde by that swerde that he shall nat be longe hole afftir. And I woll that ye weyte that thys same day shall the adventure of the Sankgreall begynne, that ys called the holy vessell.'

(Chapter 3) 'Now, fayre nevew', seyde the kynge unto sir Gawayne, 'assay ye for my love.'

Direct speech, if impassioned or rhetorical, seems indeed a favourite medieval way to begin a chapter; and in this work a chapter will also often end on a speech, particularly if it is followed by action which will make a rousing start to the following chapter.

Fairly often Caxton makes a new chapter at a dramatic point in the story, using the 'to-be-continued-in-our-next' technique. This is not particularly logical and is usually unexpected, but is justified by the effect produced. A charming example of this tantalizing sort of chapter division, and one which is refreshingly unbloodthirsty—battle scenes usually follow these dramatic pauses—occurs at Chapters 38/39 of Book X when Alys La Beale Pellaron and Sir Alysaundir Le Orphelin are making themselves known to each other.

Whan La Beale Alys sawe hym juste so well, she thought hym a passyng goodly knyght on horsebacke. And than she lepe oute of hir pavylyon and toke sir Alysaundir by the brydyll and thus she seyde: "Fayre knyght! of thy knyghthode shew me thy vysayge. 'That dare I well', seyde sir Alysayndir, 'shew my vysayge'. And than he put of his helme, and whan she sawe his vysage she sayde, 'A, swete Fadir Jesu! the I muste love, and never othir'. 'Than shew me youre vysage', seyde he'. (Chapter 39) And anone she unwympeled her, and whan he sawe her he seyde, 'A, Lorde Jesu! Here have I founde my love and my lady!'

About half a dozen times a chapter is ended, seemingly deliberately, with a tantalizing reference to a new incident which is not enlarged upon till the succeeding chapter. An example is at Chapters 12/13 of Book XXI (Caxton's text only is available here). Lancelot's funeral rites are described:

& euer his vysage was layed open & naked that al folkes myght beholde hym/for suche was the custom in tho dayes that all men of worshyp shold so lye wyth open vysage tyl that they were buryed/ [logical place for chapter to end] and ryght thus as they were at theyr seruyce there came syr Ector de maris that had vij yere sought al Englond Scotland and walys sekying his brother syr Launcelot/ Capitulum xiii And whan syr Ector herde suche noyse & lyghte in the quyre of Ioyous garde he alyght. . . .

In order that his chapters might be of reasonably uniform length Caxton was forced to make many divisions at places where at most a new paragraph seems appropriate. His material was often intractable, and some fifty of his divisions are open to criticism. Inordinately long or short chapters are found (Chapters 3 of Book I, 18 of Book IV 2 and 3 of Book V). Logical pauses are ignored, such, for example, as the end of the clearly marked episode of Sir Alysaundir Le Orphelin, which occurs in the *middle* of Chapter 40 of Book X.

Chapters occasionally stop between a question and answer, or in mid-conversation when there seems no dramatic or other reason for it. At Chapters 1/2 of Book VIII the division is actually in the middle of a sentence: 'And whan they sye that she was dede and undirstode none othir but that the kynge was destroyed' [Chapter 2] 'than sertayne of them wolde have slayne the chylde.' As for the division of Chapters 4/5 of Book XXI, it seems almost incredible that it could have been intentional: '"Therefore be my rede" seyde sir Lucan, "hit ys beste that we brynge you to som towne." "I wolde it were so", seyde the kynge, [chapter 5] but I may nat stonde, my hede worchys so"'.... It is no excuse that Chapter 4 ends towards the bottom of a page, as there is plenty of blank space.

While considering the actual appearance and presentation

of the two texts, we may include some mention of the differences in their punctuation. (These will not strike the reader nowadays, because in his edition of the Winchester MS. Professor Vinaver has introduced modern stops and layout, although happily he has not imposed too much on the manuscript's very light pointing.) Few editors seem able to leave their authors' punctuation as they find it; and Caxton was probably no exception.

Early punctuation was based more on the rhythms of speech than on logical sentence-construction, as it is today. The pointing of the Winchester MS. is of the simplest kind, and no regular stops, such as are described a little later by Aldus, are to be found here. Both scribes use only these marks in the MS.: the stroke [//], the point or full stop [.] and the capital letter. The stroke is always followed by a capital letter and sometimes by a small space. It does not occur often and always indicates a pronounced pause; but many obvious pauses are not marked at all in the MS. The most usual marks are the point and the capital letter, either together or separately: they seem interchangeable, and indicate pauses of any length, varying from those now indicated by a full stop to those suggested by a modern comma (except where they are used on either side of numerals or purely for emphasis, as after proper names).

Sentences are separated from each other, but even in long sentences containing subordinate clauses there is little internal punctuation. In conversation, speeches are pointed apart from each other but not from the 'he saids' which belong to them.

Caxton's punctuation does not differ essentially from that of the MS., but there is considerably more of it. For nearly all the books he published, including the Malory, he uses the following points, in order of weight: a paragraph mark, a space, and the stroke (/). This last is the most usual mark: the first two are often used together, and are always followed by a capital letter. Capitals sometimes occur after the strokes, and sometimes on their own, when they seem to represent something between space and stroke. The paragraph marks seem to be used at random, for one chapter will contain as many as seven or eight of them, some perhaps used to separate the speeches in a conversation, while another similar chapter will have none at all. The spaces also occur spasmodically, sometimes at a significant pause or important speech, but often where no special emphasis seems called for. The stroke, with or without the capital, seems to be used rather less at random, and marks fairly regularly some at any rate of the pauses where modern punctuation would be used. Sentences are always pointed apart with the stroke; and it also appears as the equivalent of the comma for light internal pointing, especially before *and* and *but*, and to mark adverbial, but not always noun or adjectival, clauses. Speech is usually more heavily pointed than narrative, and this is especially noticeable in impassioned or rhetorical speech where dramatic pauses, not necessarily logical ones, are often given pointing. Lists of proper names and numerals are always marked with strokes between each item.

In both texts this light pointing makes the sense perfectly clear if the passage be read aloud, and the punctuation marks in speeches seem to be designed with this in mind. But Caxton's punctuation is markedly more modern—although his symbols are unfamiliar and his longer stops somewhat arbitrarily used.

Differences between the presentation and appearance of the two versions lead one naturally to the differences of spelling, grammar, and syntax. The two former categories are considered in detail in the Appendix, where it will be seen that a comparison allows us to draw a few tentative inferences as to the region of origin of the MS. It is probably to be located somewhere further north and west than Caxton's London, though certainly not beyond the Midlands, or the variations would have been more numerous and striking. As Malory was himself a Warwickshire man, it is likely that Winchester does represent rather more closely than Caxton the actual language of the author.

No such deductions as to origins or dialects can be drawn from a comparison of the syntax of the two versions, but the differences which do exist perhaps shed some light on Caxton as editor and stylist.

While there are very few variations in verb constructions, there is no doubt that Caxton uses participial constructions far more than does the Winchester version. Sometimes these constructions get rid of repetitious *ands* and in general their use makes a neat sentence-link. For example, the MS. reads: 'There cam by them the fayreste knyght and the semelyest man that ever they sawe. But he made the grettyst dole that ever man made' (*Works*, p. 163, l. 36). Caxton reads: 'there cam by them the fayrest knyght and the semelyest man that euer they sawe/makynge the grettest dole that euer man made.'

The use (often lax) of tenses is similar in both texts, but on the whole Caxton is more logical in his ordering of sequence, especially where he substitutes the pluperfect for the preterite in indirect speech. Indeed usually indirect speech is more distinctly separated from direct speech in the print than in the MS. There are far more confusions on this point in the Malory than in Caxton's other works, and where he shows a 'better' reading he was probably trying to improve a text very faulty in this respect.

Again, agreement between verb and subject, frequently disregarded in both versions, is more often correct in Caxton than in W, which is very prone to use, for example, *there is*, *there was* followed by a plural subject.

A fondness for auxiliary verbs reveals Caxton as a laboured stylist. In his text but not in the MS. there are many examples of the intrusive *do*, in particular, and also of *lete*, *make*, and *go*. In a typical case W reads 'Merlion dud hys mayster Bloyse wryte them. Also he dud wryte . . .' (*Works*, p. 38, l. 3): while Caxton has 'merlyn dyd his maister Bleyse do wryte/Also he did do wryte. . . .".

There still remain, after the variations which bear on spelling, phonology, or grammar have been noted, the great bulk of the variants that swell Professor Vinaver's footnotes. Can anything be deduced from them as to the relative accuracy of the two texts, or their stylistic merits? Or are there anywhere signs of conscious glossing or modernizing?

Many of the variations can be shown to be nothing more

than scribal errors; and of these most are the homoeoteleuta, or accidental omissions, which have caused many corrupt passages. Where there is doubt references to the French originals can often show which reading is correct: elsewhere one version may be so much fuller or more circumstantial as to be obviously genuine Malory. Variations of this sort have been carefully and expertly analysed by Professor Vinaver, whose conclusions one may safely accept.

As for the accuracy of the two texts, examination of the incidence of homoeoteleuta, the errors most easily detected, shows that clear cases of this fault are three times more numerous in the Winchester MS. than in Caxton's print. In the cases of other corruptions where a guide is supplied by the original French, Caxton shows nearly twice as many correct readings. Either Caxton's copy was superior to the Winchester scribes', or he followed it more carefully; both circumstance may have obtained; in any case, had we only the Winchester text to go on, we should find ourselves more frequently puzzled by its readings than we were by Caxton's when his was the only available version.

There are also many passages where Caxton provides a more grammatical reading (I am not referring now to the constant differences of usage, but to mechanical accuracy). Small additions or omissions, or the altering of conjunctions, provide clearer, more regular sentences so often that mere chance seems unlikely; as it does in the many cases where the sense is just a shade more explicit in Caxton: cf. e.g. W's: 'Merlion dud make kynge Arthur that sir Gawayne was sworne to telle . . .' (*Works*, p. 108) with Caxton's: 'merlyn desyred of kyng Arthur that Syre Gauayne shold be sworne . . .&c.'

There are a very large number of places where inessential words or phrases are left out or small alterations and rearrangements made in Caxton's text. These do not at all obscure the sense, and in many instances were probably deliberate, as the resulting readings are neater, e.g. 'he descended downe from hys horse' becomes simply 'descended from'.

Ján Šimko, in his recent study, based mainly on Book V,

of Word Order in the two texts,[1] notes that throughout the rest of the material 'we also find differences (of word order), but they seem to be rather the result of a routine procedure of changing or modernizing the text occasionally, not systematically'. Caxton, he finds, shows a preference for the usual modern sentence order—'Subject—Finite Verb—Predicate or other Material'. Winchester's word order tends to be freer.

In spite of so many preferable readings Caxton's clearer and more grammatical text does suffer in some places from overmuch minor omission; and also from the repetition of certain words, and the use of double adjectives: these faults have all the same tendency, which is to flatten Malory's very individual style, although sense and syntax are unaffected.

The repetitions and pairs of double adjectives (or occasionally nouns or verbs)—'doublets'—in Caxton's text may imply no more than that his copy was to blame or that the Winchester scribes have omitted redundant words. However, the evidence of Caxton's own style, as it is seen, for example, in the Preface to this and other books published by him, shows that he was given to wordiness and formality: it is possible that some of the phrases which seem to us like 'padding' may have actually been inserted by him. There are no fewer than fifty-seven pairs of adjectives (of the 'great and myghty', 'worship and honour' type) in his text where in W only one, or (rarely) neither, of the pair is to be found. (There are, it is true, eighteen cases of the converse, but four of these can be explained by contamination from alliterative sources.) Some cases may of course represent accidental omissions in one or other text.

Some of the instances where the complete pair has been added to Caxton's version suggest that the text is corrupt, and that the passage containing the doublet may represent actual re-writing. Examination of Book V reveals case after case of this trick of style in passages where Caxton is re-wording his text. Certain doublets, or words in them, recur frequently; e.g. 'worship and honour', 'renoume',

[1] *Word-Order in the Winchester Manuscript and in William Caxton's Edition of Thomas Malory's 'Morte Darthur'* (1485) *A Comparison*; Halle, 1957.

'noble', which have a chivalric ring; other pairs have a formal or legal tone—'agree and consente', 'charge yow and commaunde yow' (in both instances only the first word of the pair appears in W).

There are a number of interesting variants between single words. Some words found in W were, at the time when Caxton was printing, obsolete, or nearly so, or gallicisms or dialect forms: many of these are rendered in the printed text by more modern forms or counterparts. Some of these alterations look like deliberate modernizations and were very probably made by Caxton himself, especially as some variants have the dignified or Latinate tone so typical of his style. Very few words remain in the printed text which are not immediately intelligible to the modern reader; this cannot be said of the MS.

It is not surprising to find very many such variants in Book V, where Caxton was re-working his copy, but they occur throughout the rest of the volume as well. Some of them may be the result of corruption in one or both texts, or of misunderstandings, and occasionally it is W that has the more modern reading, but this is rare. I do not propose to give examples of the curious forms and words in both texts which have obviously been caused by confusions, mistakes, or misunderstanding; but a few quotations will give a sufficiently clear idea of the apparently conscious corrections, standardizations, and modernizations to be found in Caxton.

Thus, where Winchester uses the word *thirl*, a predominantly northern word normally meaning 'pierce', in the otherwise unrecorded sense of 'trickle' or 'pour'—'their blode thirled downe to their feete' (p. 106, l. 6)—Caxton replaces it by *renne*, which makes perfect sense and is the regular English of his day. Again, at that time even more than now the use of *frende* as a verb was unusual, and where it occurs in the MS.—'he woll so frende hym' (p. 427 l. 15)—Caxton's text reads 'he wylle get him such frendes'.

An interesting variant, which seems to show Caxton shying away from an unfamiliar northern word, occurs when W reads (of knights preparing to charge); 'they toke their bere' (*W* 323, l. 13) and the print has 'they toke their renne'. *Bere* is derived from Old Norse, *byrr*, and while not especially rare in the North (occurring several times in alliterative verse), in this exact sense of 'run-up' it does not appear at all often, and it seems likely that Caxton deliberately substituted a form of the familiar 'run'. Again, the rare *thirstelew* ('very thirsty') is replaced by *moche thursty* in Caxton's version. *Dwere*, which occurs twice in W and was apparently out of date in Caxton's day, is replaced in the printed text on each occasion by its exact equivalent *doubt*. The verb *boten*, 'to heal', used impersonally, *it boteneth not*), appears twice in W: this also is a comparatively rare and early word, and Caxton justifiably substitutes *help*.

A marked gallicism, which occurs three times and is each time altered, is *play*, rendered by Caxton *wound*. Similarly, *pouste*, a French word lingering only in Scotland, becomes *power* in the print. One or two legal or technical terms (usually chivalric) which had become unfamiliar or obsolescent are also given in a more up-to-date form for Caxton's readers.

The actual forms of certain words (apart from the variations already noted in the forms of some verbs) also show some variations between the texts, and some of these are constant. The MS. usually shows the forms *other*, *nother* and *whother*, while Caxton has *or*, *nor* and *wheder* or *whether*: it sometimes uses *nat* ('not') in the sense of 'nothing', and *none* for 'not'. All these variants in the MS. are somewhat older than Caxton's forms, and some went out of use at about this date. Another word always found in a different form in Caxton's text is *spiteuously*, which was apparently little used at this time (the last quotation in the *Oxford Dictionary* is for 1481), and which always becomes *piteously*, or, once, *spitefully*, in the print.

Certain variations can only be explained, and at that tentatively, by supposing Caxton to have had a preference for, or aversion from, particular words; for no logical reasons, such as a wish to modernize his text, seem to account for the alterations. Several of these occur two or three times, and whereas a single change may be laid to the pen of an unconscientious scribe, those which are repeated and invariable suggest that someone was showing conscious preferences. That this person was Caxton cannot of course be proven, but the predilection for a formal, even pompous vocabulary which is noticeable in his other writing seems consistent with what appears in these alterations.

We find, for example, *broughte vnder* substituted for *wrothe* (twisted) *undir*, *halp vp* for *hove up*, *truage* for *bondage*, *surgeons* for *lechecrafte*, *richesse* for *gyftes*, *endured* for *helde on*, and *lyffte up* for *heve up*. In this list it can be seen that on the whole Caxton's substitutions show a partiality for Romance forms and lack vividness.

Among the variations which occur several times are *nourrysh*, replacing *fostir*, *grete* or *gretely*, replacing various equivalents and sometimes added without precedent, like *fair*, which is sprinkled all over Caxton's text.

It is difficult to arrive at a conclusion when trying to assess the stylistic merits of the two texts, even when the term 'style' is stretched to cover syntax and vocabulary. Where large-scale variations are so rare (with the exception of Book V), arrangement of phrasing perhaps does most to form one's impressions, and in this respect it is hardly possible to say that one text is consistently more felicitous than the other. Caxton's version might be held to be a little superior in general accuracy, and in neatness and compactness of sentence, and for the average modern reader his language is easier: but on the other hand he sometimes lacks liveliness. And his text is blemished by a few omissions so glaring and puzzling that they deserve separate mention.[1]

In two cases what is lost in Caxton's version is a rare touch of personal emotion. The first of these two occurs during the last speech of the dying Elaine of Astolat to her confessor: this speech begins as follows in the MS. (*W* 1093)

Than she seyde, 'Why sholde I leve such thoughtes? Am I nat an erthely woman? And all the whyle the brethe ys in my body I may complayne me, for my belyve ys that I do none offence, though I love

[1] An omission in the first book (*W* 22. 24–25), is concerning Arthur's reception of some visiting Kings, hardly comes within this category: here Caxton may have been pruning a non-essential—or working from a faulty copy. In his otherwise careful text it is very unlikely that any passage could have suffered so much by accident.

an erthely man, unto God, for He fourmed me thereto, and all maner of good love comyth of God. And othir than good love loved I never sir Launcelot du Lake. And I take God to recorde, I loved never none but hym, nor never shall, of erthely creature; and a clene maydyn I am for hym and for all othir.'

In Caxton the clause in which Elaine asserts her belief that earthly love is indeed ordained by God is omitted. He may have felt it to be controversial; he leaves out some other references to God in his version of Book V.

His text runs:

thenne she sayd why shold I leue suche thoughtes/am I not an erthely woman/and alle the whyle the brethe is in my body I may compleyne me/for my byleue is I doo none offence/though I loue an erthely man/and I take god to my recorde I loued neuer none but syr Launcelot du Lake nor neuer shall/and a clene mayden I am for hym and for alle other.

The rest of the speech is almost identical in both versions.

Gawain's dying speech to Arthur has suffered even more severely—as may be seen by comparing the two texts as they appear on p. 1230 of the *Works*. What is lost in Caxton's version, which does admittedly give a précis of the essentials, is again the sharply idiosyncratic element, represented here by a confession of guilt and fallibility. It seems extremely likely that here, for whatever reason, Caxton has done some editing; for his compact rendering, relying on many of the words found in his MS. version (e.g. *thorow*, *causer*) stands in comparison with his presumed original exactly as do the re-written passages in Book V. To these we must now turn.

This extraordinary Book, based on the English alliterative poem *Morte Arthure* is so unlike the others 'drawyn from the Frensshe' that one is inclined to accept Professor Vinaver's theory that it was written before them. In the original romance many knights appear whose names mean nothing in the French stories: battles not only between principals but minor characters are described in stroke-by-stroke detail, and speeches of heroic length and temper constantly interrupt the action. For this Book to have been at all comparable with his other seven, Malory would have had to reduce it from the original twice as much as he had already done. It was left to Caxton to do this, and also to remove much of the unusual vocabulary and style which Malory took over from his source. The style indeed is in even more marked contrast than the material to the rest of the volume. Whole lines of verse are often found unaltered, inversions and alliteration abound, and the vocabulary is strongly poetic as well as being distinctly northern.

It is true that Caxton does not state explicitly in his Preface that he has cut down this book by half: but the evidence of style suggests that it was he who was responsible. The chief difference in style between Caxton's Book V and his other twenty books is not, as is usually supposed, the fact that marked traces of alliterative and poetic language still show, but that the narrative is written in a manner far less flowing and lively, far more formal and sophisticated. A point-by-point investigation of his changes is justified, if only because it shows us what were his aims, preferences, and prejudices.

The Book opens with Arthur holding a feast and 'Table Round'. To him enter messengers from Lucius, the Roman emperor, who is demanding tribute. Caxton alters their opening address to more courteous and general terms, omits altogether a scene where the messengers quail before Arthur's angry looks, and proceeds directly to the demand for 'trewage'. Arthur's lengthy reply is reduced to a line and a half of indirect speech. The subsequent entertainment of the messengers is described, but briefly.

The early and more important speeches in Arthur's council of war are fairly fully reported in Caxton, but later speeches are reduced to a summary of the number of men each speaker can supply for the campaign. At the end of the council the Romans are given their answer, and one speech from Arthur and some *oratio obliqua* replace several speeches in the MS.

Caxton indicates the return route of the messengers, dropping some details. Their report and Lucius' speeches on hearing it are somewhat altered in phrasing, but they contain salient features of Roman policy, and presumably for this reason Caxton does not reduce them much; he also keeps in some detail the list of Lucius' allies.

Caxton's third chapter, describing Arthur's embarkation, is compressed from the original, but only a few details and some redundant or alliterative phrases are actually omitted. The vocabulary and word order of the strongly alliterative passage describing Arthur's dream of the dreadful dragon are slightly altered by Caxton, but all the detail remains. This episode could have been left out without affecting the story, but perhaps it appealed to Caxton; as also may have the ensuing incident of the giant's abdication of the Duchess of Brittany, in which only one speech is reduced to *oratio obliqua*.

When Arthur approaches the giant's lair, many details of arming, horsemanship, and so on are left out, but the conversation between Arthur and the Duchess' nurse is but little abridged. It is noticeable that Arthur's address to the giant is shorn of most of its oaths and abuse (and this is true of many other speeches in Caxton's version). All details of the giant's appearance are cut out. The actual fight, already well adapted by Malory from his source, is further shortened by Caxton; and he makes the combat perhaps less heroic but certainly less revolting by omitting detailed descriptions of the various strokes, though the total number of injuries is much the same in both versions. Many of the details omitted from this scene are strongly alliterative.

The jests of Arthur and Bedivere about the alleged 'corsaint' are omitted by Caxton: he may have felt them to be blasphemous as well as irrelevant. Arthur's arrangements for the disposal of the body, and his references to another giant he had previously slain are kept, but much else is cut. The scene in which the populace learn of the giant's death is shortened, but the gist of Arthur's reply to their eulogies —that thanks are due only to God—is not obscured in Caxton's version.

The speech in which the Marshal of France describes Lucius' depredations, and Arthur's reply are both abridged. General description of the embassage of Bors and Gawain to the Emperor is fairly full, but Caxton cuts severely the heroic alliterative speeches on this occasion though direct speech is kept. Pruning of all but dramatic essentials of the interview makes the scene actually more striking in Caxton's version.

Caxton begins his really ruthless compression during the fighting which then follows. His policy is to make but the briefest mention of knights present during this campaign only, thus focusing attention on characters who are already known or who are later to play a major part in this or other Books. This has the effect of knitting Book V more closely to the rest of the work. Speeches during battles, and details of particular encounters and actual strokes dealt are often cut clean away. In this engagement the only speeches left intact are two spoken by Gawain: Arthur's orders and their fulfilment are reduced to absolute essentials. Conversations between a British advance party and a Roman ambush, and between the former and Lancelot are omitted, and Caxton merely records that they 'retorned and told syr Launcelot that there lay in a wayte for them thre score thousand Romayns'. In the ensuing battle pages of detailed description are cut to a few lines recording the dead and a few more telling of the prowess of Lancelot. When the story returns to Arthur, however, less is cut and his speeches stand almost intact.

Again, when in Caxton's next chapter (viii) the scene changes to the Roman camp, Lucius' speech to his army, though somewhat altered, and transposed to an earlier and more logical place in the narrative, is kept at much its original length; but the battle following is drastically reduced. The following words are all that remain in Caxton's version, and it must be admitted that they cover the action quite adequately:

> Thenne the batails approuched and shoue and showted on bothe sydes and grete strokes were smyten on bothe sydes/many men ouerthrowen/hurte/& slayn and grete valyaunces/prowesses and appertyces of werre were that day shewed/whiche were ouer long to recounte the noble feates of euery man/For they shold conteyne an hole volume.

An account of Arthur's personal bravery is then brought forward from a passage the rest of which Caxton cuts, and as everything else has been so much compressed this reference to Arthur acquires new prominence. The next incidents, Arthur's slaying of the giant Galapas and the Emperor Lucius in single combats, are similarly emphasized by being less cut than the surrounding matter. The lengthy episode when Sir Kay is wounded is omitted altogether, and the final rout of the Romans is reduced to general terms; but Arthur's care of his wounded, his preparations for the funeral of Lucius and the dead senators, and the message to be carried to Rome by the surviving senators are all described with some detail, and the scene when these senators arrive in Rome with their sad tidings is even somewhat longer in Caxton's version.

Caxton again cuts severely, though some pretty details are allowed to remain, at the beginning of his next chapter; this describes Arthur's progress into Italy, and includes in W a number of irrelevant (and very alliterative) conversations. The episode of Sir Gawain and Sir Priamus is allowed by Caxton to stand very much as in W, though with some altered phrasing; probably because though not strictly relevant to the action, it, like Arthur's dragon dream, is interesting in itself and centres on a well-known figure. Later on, some strongly alliterative speeches, dealing in part with tactics and prospects for the next engagement are turned to *oratio obliqua* or omitted altogether.

This battle scene is reduced less than previous ones, and some combats and conversations involving Gawain, Priamus, and Florence, though abbreviated, are not removed. The less relevant incident of the death of Gawain's ward Chastelayne is much abridged, and no mention is made of some obscure knights who figure in W at this point. The last stages of the battle are also shortened and the knights' announcement of the victory to Arthur becomes *oratio obliqua*.

Many details, especially some alliterative speeches, are removed from the descriptions of Arthur's assault on the 'Tuscan city', and the same is true of the subsequent progress to 'Urbyne'. A comprehensive précis is given by Caxton of the W's highly alliterative description of the conquest of this city. He partially re-writes the account of Arthur's coronation by the Pope, but it is not much abbreviated; though Arthur's gifts of land to his knights are not mentioned. The conversation between Arthur and the knights, which results in the return of the army to Britain, is also reworded, but kept at the same length as the original. This scene concludes the campaign and the book.

This survey shows clearly that when Caxton is cutting the first things to go are detailed battle descriptions, the exploits of unknown knights, heroic speeches: all of which obscure what he conceived to be the important events and characters of the story. The main thread of the narrative is allowed to show more plainly in Caxton's conciser version, occasionally the sense is actually improved, and in only one instance do minor confusions (mostly geographical) result from excessive compression.

Details that Caxton finds worth preserving are those which concern the progress of the war—messengers' speeches, statements of policy—and especially episodes in which Arthur, Lancelot, or Gawain are protagonists: this is shown by the full version of Arthur's dream and the Gawain-Priamus fight. In some places in the battle-scenes material is rearranged to imply that the parts played by certain knights, particularly Arthur and Lancelot, were outstanding and decisive, whereas the poem and the Winchester version may not give this impression at all. Contrary to some opinions, Caxton's selective text enhances rather than detracts from Arthur's glory.

From the type of material Caxton kept in—or even added to—his version over and above the bare necessities of the story, we may guess at some of his editorial—and perhaps personal—likes and dislikes. This material falls with gratifying readiness into two or three main categories.

Passages relating to rank, title, dignity, courtesy form a large part of it. For example, the messengers from Rome address Arthur as follows in W: 'the gretis welle Lucius the Emperour of Roome', but in Caxton's text this grows to 'The hyghe and myghty Emperour Lucyus sendeth to the kyng of Bretayne gretyng'. This somewhat pompous strain continues throughout Caxton's version of the speech. Again, though much surrounding matter is reduced, the following reference to Arthur stands in its original length in the printed text: 'Syr ye oughte of ryght to be aboue al other kynges/for vnto yow is none lyke ne pareylle in Christendome/of knyghthode ne of dygnyte.'

In view of this attitude to rank and sovereignty it may seem a little surprising that Caxton omits the lines in W which state 'there shall never harlot have happe by the helpe of oure Lord, to kylle a crowned kynge that with creme is anoynted'. But this markedly alliterative passage occurs during a deleted conversation; and no other instance suggests that he had the slightest wish to minimize either the temporal or spiritual prestige of the monarchy. On the contrary, shortly after this passage Caxton inserts, with no apparent justification in his original: 'That noble conqueroure Arthur/For his myght & prowesse is most to be doubted seen the noble kynges and grete multytude of knyghtes of the round table to whome none erthely prynce may compare.' Nor, incidentally, was Caxton oblivious of the peculiar significance of 'creme', the sacramental oil and balm, nor of the rites of coronation, for in the appropriate place he is careful to include references to them: cf. *W* 244-5.

The chivalric ideals of honour and courtesy are by no means obscured in Caxton's text, in spite of the ruthless cutting of many 'heroic' speeches. He preserves, for example, the passage in which Arthur rebukes the young knights who would have fallen on the Roman messengers who had spoken slightingly of the king—'For the Romayns ben grete lordes and though theyr message please me not ne my courte yet I must remembre myn honour.' The chivalrous attitude to ladies is illustrated by this speech, hardly abbreviated in Caxton's text, which Arthur addresses to the Countess of a captured city: 'thene the Kynge aualed his vyser with a meke & noble countenance/and said madame ther shal none of my subgettys mysdoo you ne your maydens/ne to none that to yow longen.' Many small details—Gawain going 'in the spryngynge of the day . . . to seke some aduentures' references to honour and courage not deleted from otherwise much mutilated speeches, descriptions of silken pavilions in a meadow, the arms on a shield—contribute to the effect which surely Caxton of all people would want to preserve, he who in the much-quoted lament over the decay of English knighthood (in his Preface to the *Feates of Armes*) so plainly hankered after a chivalric past. His omission of much more such material is certainly not because he lacked sympathy with it, but because of the necessity for reduction and for achieving a less alliterative effect. Where opportunity to use such matter arises he almost always profits by it.

Another sort of material that seems to have attracted Caxton was the moral and religious. I have already noted how he has removed the joking reference to the giant of St. Michael's as a 'corsaint', and another brief reference of the same kind also goes. After the giant's death Arthur's pious thanksgivings were more to Caxton's taste, for he includes the sentence that reads as follows in his text: 'And he sayd ageyne yeue the thanke to god/and departe the goodes among yow/And after that kynge Arthur sayd and commaunded his Cosyn howel that he shold ordeyne for a chirche to be bylded on the same hylle in the worship of saynte Mychel.' Several other brief references to religious matters are preserved in the printed version, and though not striking in themselves they acquire significance simply because they have escaped wholesale cutting.

A Christian touch which seems to have been added by Caxton to a speech by Gawain, together with the fact that references to 'Sarasyns' are almost always left intact in his text, prompts the thought that Caxton may have wanted to encourage the view of the campaign against Rome as a sort of crusade, a holy war which could be related to the later mystical Christianity of the Grail story. The speech given to Gawain runs as follows: 'Wherfore I aduyse to take our armes and to make vs redy to mete with these sarasyns and mysbyleuyng men/and wyth the helpe of god we shal ouerthrowe them and haue a fayre day on them.'

There are also some examples in Caxton's text of a tendency to moralize, not altogether surprising when one remembers the Preface to the *Morte Darthur* with its exhortations to its readers to 'Doo after the good and leue the euyl/and it shal brynge you to good fame and renommee'. There is, for instance, no parallel in W for 'it shall be ensamble perpetual vnto alle kynges and prynces/for to deny their truage vnto that noble empyre' (this speech is put into the mouth of an enemy but the tone is distinctly Caxtonian); or for the messenger's caustic remark to Lucius: 'I fere me ye haue made a rodde for yourself.' Nor does Caxton omit from one of Arthur's speeches the words 'and for to tempte god it is no wysedome', though he does remove the preceding sentence 'inowghe is as good as a feste'.

Professor Vinaver has observed that Malory possessed an eye for the mundane and mercenary things of life. From the evidence of Book V, this faculty seems to have been even better developed in Caxton. There is not a single passage in the MS. relating to treasure, money, or any financial transaction which is not reproduced by Caxton in his version. Indeed, he even appears to have added this clause to Arthur's orders for the conduct of his army while on the Continent: 'that noo man in payne of dethe shold not robbe ne take vytaylle /ne other thynge by the way but that he shold paye therfore.' This sentence is a good example of Caxton's somewhat legalistic style, here quite appropriate, and also strengthens his representation of Arthur as a just and merciful conqueror. Caxton also makes Arthur give the Roman messengers 'grete and large yeftes' and pay 'alle theyr dispencys', whereas in the poem and W they are summarily sent packing.

Caxton's choice of what to keep and what to omit brings his Book V much more in line with his other twenty than the MS. version is with the other seven parts of the Winchester text. The style of his version continues the standardizing process; the passages he re-writes completely may be a little formal or flat, but for most of the book his skilful re-wording and well-judged omissions break the alliteration and tame the uncouth language into something much more compatible with Malory's normal style than is the MS. version. This is so even in the précis of the battles, or in certain scenes at court, where the greater complexity of the sentences, occasionally stilted 'business English', pairs of nearly synonymous words, or Latinate vocabulary seem unmistakably the work of the editor. It is noticeable that these characteristics are most marked on formal occasions, and when there is plenty of action and drama Caxton relies much more on the phraseology and language of the original.

Simko's detailed study of word order in Book V, already

mentioned, shows that there is a strong tendency for any other word order in Winchester to be replaced by the more regular subject—verb—predicate order in Caxton's text. Where, sometimes, the pattern is reversed and Caxton shows an inversion of this order, this is often due to his wish 'to use as far as possible the objective order Theme-Nucleus', i.e. to start his phrase with the previously stated 'theme' under discussion, even if this happens to be in an oblique case. Simko concludes that frequent use of the modern, regular word order, combined with the tendency to shape the sentence according to its semantic demands, tends to smooth down Winchester's 'frequent effusions of liveliness', and to make Caxton's version more polished.

An excellent example of Caxton's formal style, where he is indeed adding to his book, is found in his version of Arthur's reply to the Roman messengers. The two versions read together bring irresistibly to mind the scene in *Henry V* when Henry delivers his stirring challenge to the French throne, which is then followed by the Archbishops' dry-as-dust exposition of Henry's legal rights thereto. Nevertheless, Caxton's reading, however it may lose in liveliness, is certainly more 'standard' English and is not entirely incongruous in the context.

The MS. reads (*W* 190.15):

'Hit is well', seyde the kynge. 'Now sey ye to youre Emperour that I shall in all haste me redy make with my keene knyghtes, and by the rever of Rome holde my Rounde Table. And I woll brynge with me the beste peple of fyftene realmys, and with hem ryde on the mountaynes in the maynelondis, and myne downe the wallys of Myllayne the proude, and syth ryde unto Roome with my royallyst knyghtes Now ye have youre answere, hygh you that ye were hense. . . .'

For this Caxton has:

And in presence of alle his lordes and knyghtes he sayd to them in thys wyse/I wylle that ye retorne vnto your lord and procurour of the comyn wele for the Romayns/and saye ye to hym Of his demaunde and commaundement I sette nothyng/And that I knowe of no truage ne trybute that I owe to hym/ne to none erthely prynce/Crysten ns hethen/but I pretende to haue and to occupye the souerayne of thempyre/wherin I am entytled by the ryght of my predecessoure somtyme kynges of this lond/and saye to hym that I am delybered and fully concluded to goo wyth myn armye with strengthe and power vnto Rome by the grace of god to take possession in thempyre/and subdue them that ben rebelle/wherfore I commaunde hym and alle them of Rome that incontynent they make to me their homage or to knouleche me for their Emperour and gouernour vpon payne that shal ensiewe. . . .

This passage is a very extreme example of Caxton's style, but the same tendency to formality is found throughout his version of Book V: 'demaunded of her wherfore she made suche lamentacion' for W's 'asked hir why she sate sorowing' is fairly typical of many reworded phrases.

It must not be supposed that defects of prolixity, pomposity, or repetition mar Caxton's style throughout this book: they are far outweighed by the positive virtues of clarity and conciseness which are more commonly met with. When constructing his composite sentences from an original passage perhaps twice as long, he uses the technique of discerning selection with the same success which enabled him to produce in his Book a brief but accurate summary of the actual events of this Tale. Excellent examples of this technique abound, and one passage in particular which shows, at rather too great length for quotation here, almost every one of Caxton's devices for abbreviation, is to be found in Vinaver's edition on p. 235. It describes the preparations for a local engagement: in Caxton's version a whole speech by one obscure knight is omitted, as are some details of his attributes, without altering any material particulars of the episode. Details of the strategy of, and the numbers involved in, the skirmish are kept. Speeches by the principal characters concerned are stripped of alliterative phrases, and synonyms are substituted for single alliterating words, yet much of the language of the original remains, and with it not only the purport of the speeches but the chivalric ideals which permeate the passage.

A shorter passage that shows Caxton dealing in typical manner with poetic and alliterative material comes from the battle between Gawain and Priamus, and shows not only how he omits some details and alters others, but how he substitutes narrative for direct speech. W reads:

'Now fecche me', seyde sir Pryamus, 'my vyall that hangys by the gurdyll of my haynxman, for hit is full of the floure of the four good watyrs that passis from Paradyse, the mykyll fruyte in fallys that at one day fede shall us all. Putt that watir in oure fleysh where the syde is tamed, and we shall be hole within four houres'. Than they lette clense their woundys with colde whyght wyne, and than they lete anoynte them with bawme over and over, and holer men than they were within an houres space was never lyvyng syn God the worlde made.'

Caxton reduces this to:

And pryamus toke fro his page a vyolle ful of the four waters that came oute of paradys/and with certayne baume enoynted theyr woundes/ and wesshe them with that water/& within an houre after/they were both as hole as euer they were.

Here are no *gurdyll*, *floure*, *mykyll fruyte* or *cold whyght wyne*; the alliterating *haynxman* and *passis* become *page* and *came*; the last sentence is quite reworked: and yet the sense remains substantially the same, nor is the miraculous element lost.

Rearrangement, linking of sentences by the use of conjunctions, participial constructions, and *oratio obliqua* are some other means used by Caxton to reduce material that he does not wish to delete completely. The use of indirect speech makes easier the elimination of alliterative details; and where, as so frequently happens, Arthur's orders to his army or knights are thus rendered, the result is the happy one of giving Arthur still more dignity, for 'he commanded them to do' is more absolute than 'he said to them "Do this". . . .'

Although, as we have seen, strongly alliterative material is often removed in bulk, short alliterating phrases are excised or rearranged, and single alliterating words replaced by synonyms, yet Caxton has left in his version one or two complete alliterative lines (the language of none of these, however, is markedly poetic or unfamiliar), and in certain passages a good deal of alliterative matter remains. These passages are usually lively and striking in themselves, and it seems that up to a certain point Caxton did appreciate their poetic qualities. In Arthur's dragon dream, for example, which appears at some length in the print, much of the vocabulary is exactly as in the MS. and in the poem, but there are many small changes which remove both the rhythm of the verse lines and some unusual or strongly alliterating words (e.g. 'the worme wyndis away' becomes 'the dragon flewe away'): yet, as this extract describing the dragon shows, a vivid poetic flavour remains: 'And his hede was enameled with asure/and his sholders shone as gold/his bely lyke maylles of a merueyllous hewe/his taylle ful of tatters/his feet ful of fyne sable/& his clawes lyke fyne gold.' There is one curious example which shows Caxton breaking the rhythm and alliteration by actually adding words to a complete alliterative line, and incidentally creating a fine specimen of Caxtonian prose, doublets and all: where the MS. reads: 'For I was so haute in my herte I helde no men my pere', Caxton has: 'I was soo elate and hauteyn in my hert that I thought no man my pere ne to me semblable' (*W* 231.17).

Much need not be said in detail about Caxton's changes in the vocabulary of his version of Book V, for his wish to bring its language into line with that of the other books led, as we have seen, to the widespread substitution of synonyms for words which, though not all necessarily obscure or out of date, were in their context poetic, and often North-country. Of course there are instances in this book, as in the others, of changes which are probably made because the word in the Winchester text and therefore probably in Caxton's copy, was indeed dialectal and unfamiliar, or was on the point of dropping out of use. In Caxton's text we find, for instance *rugged* for *to-rongeled*, *deuyll* for *warlow*, *spryngynge* for *grekynge* (as is dawning of the day); but such cases are not here as conspicuous as they are in the rest of the volume which has been otherwise so little tampered with.

After comparing the two versions of Book V the ordinary reader is bound to decide in favour of Caxton's: nothing essential is lacking from it, while much that is tedious or incongruous is removed.

This favourable view of Caxton must extend in justice to cover the whole of his *Morte Darthur*. He has made a coherent whole from his somewhat unsophisticated original, providing his reader with an interesting explanatory preface, book and chapter divisions that are usually well-chosen, rubrics for the chapters, and reasonably consistent punctuation. Above all his text is careful and accurate; and most of what appear to be editorial liberties, especially the substitution of more modern equivalents, are either perfectly justifiable or too slight to cause serious objection. Caxton's text does not need re-editing: it is sufficiently professional to stand on its own and deserves not to be forgotten.

Linguistic comparison of the texts

The majority of the constant spelling variants between the texts prove nothing relevant to dialect or origins, and probably result mainly from preferences or whims of individual scribes. Within each text there is a great deal of haphazard spelling: final *e*, for example, is used or omitted indiscriminately and seems to have lost all trace of adjectival or adverbial force. Certain vowels are interchangeable in both texts: *y* alternates with *i* (*syr/sir*), or *u* (*dyd/dud*) or even *e* (vb. *fylle/felle*). *w* and *u* are also interchangeable (*sowle/soule*). However, in the Winchester text *i* or *y* nearly always represents Caxton's *e* in neutral final syllables (W *modir*/C *moder*).

Other constant spelling trends are: Caxton usually doubles the *o* in words where this vowel is long, such as *so*, *do*, *go*; W's spelling is *so*, etc. Caxton uses *a* forms for *land*, *hand*, while W spells such words with *o*. W spells a few words with *a* where Caxton uses *e*, for example *ascape* for *escape*, *Marlyon* for *Merlyn*, *spare* for *spere* (vb. to ask). A regular variation, which may be northern or western, is shown in W's spelling of certain words rendered by Caxton as *abasshe*, *dasshe*, *wasshe*: here the MS. spelling adds *y* after the *a*, e.g. *waysshe*.

The most interesting of the few consonantal variations are those which appear in some forms of the verb to *give*. The Winchester text usually has spellings found in the north and east Midlands which derive from Scandinavian forms, e.g. *gyftes*, *gyven*: while Caxton shows the native southerly forms *yeftes*, *yeven*. The converse occasionally appears, when Caxton produces a form like *gaf*.

As to grammatical variants, some obvious differences appear in noun plurals, which as already noted tend to show *y* rather than *e* forms in the MS. (*horsys* for *horses*), and this is true also of genitive inflections, which are spelt *-ys* or *-is* by the W scribes. This hint of a more northerly origin for the MS. is strengthened by the comparative and superlative forms of the adjective, for in the W text at least half of the forms are found to have spellings like *bettir*, *fayrist*', where Caxton has *better*, *fayrest*.

The northern comparative *werre* and its variant *warre* (from *ill*,) appear more often in the MS than in Caxton, who usually prints *worse*.

In both versions syntax is less regular than is allowed nowadays. Both, for example, show a great many double comparatives and superlatives, though there are more in the MS, which often shows the tautology where Caxton uses the simple form or even the positive. It is probable that W's fuller complement of these double forms represents what Malory wrote, and that Caxton may have eliminated many of them from his text. Double negatives also appear sometimes in W, but not in Caxton.

The pronominal forms do not differ significantly between the texts, merely showing spelling variants, all or most of which occur in both versions. Neither do the demonstrative or relative pronouns yield much of interest: W prefers *tho* (and once has the rare form *thos* while Caxton has *these*), and both texts use *that* far more often than *which*, Caxton often putting *the which* when he does use *which*. Forms of the indefinite pronoun seldom vary much between the texts: there are four instances of W's preferring the genitive plural *alther* where Caxton used *all*: Caxton prefers the form *everych* to W's *every*. Neither of these variations is very significant. As a rule the syntax of the pronoun is similar in both texts, but there is no clear case in Caxton of W's occasional use of *his* in place of the genitive inflection -'*s*.

Caxton's usage of the dative after adjectives and the verb *to be* is on the whole stricter than that of the MS.: he shows more *well was him that* . . . and fewer *well was he that* constructions than W. Again he is more successful than the MS. in dealing with the relative genitive, though both texts often fail to master this construction adequately. It is noticeable, however, that while Caxton often uses oblique cases of *who* (e.g. *to*, or *by, whom*) to replace W's clumsier *that* followed by a clause, the Winchester text shows several examples of *whos* where Caxton reads *his*: for example, *a good knyght in the land of Hungre whose name was sir Urre*, where Caxton has . . . *his name was* . . .'

The forms of both strong and weak verbs show little significant variation between the texts, both of which commonly have two or three spellings of most parts of most verbs, and often show several different forms of certain parts of some verbs. There are some interesting spellings, among them W's preterite *sye* (Caxton, *sawe*), which occurs frequently and represents an older form. The MS. also shows *chese*, *swore* and *wexed* or *woxe* for Caxton's invariable *chose*, *sware* and *waxed*.

The inflections of the present indicative are worth noting. While the first person singular is the same in both texts (usually uninflected, with a sporadic *e*), the second person singular invariably occurs in the MS. in its *-yst* or *-ist* form, while the print always has *-est*. This trend continues with W's *-yth* or *-ith*, or occasionally *-es*, *-ys* or *-is* forms of the third person singular (the latter group of spellings, definitely northern or north Midland, often occurs in impersonal verbs, e.g. *mesemys*): Caxton always has *-eth*. The influence of the alliterative *Morte Arthure*, with its markedly northern language, seems responsible for the particularly large number of these *-ys* forms in Book V.

The first and second persons plural are almost always uninflected in both texts: and so, frequently, is the third person: where inflections are found W's endings are always *-yth* or *-ith*, and Caxton's usually *-en*. The MS. form may derive from a western or southern Midland dialect, while Caxton's form, originally eastern or northern Midland, was increasingly common in London at this date.

A few northern *-and* (e) endings for the present participle occur in W's version of Book V[1]: but the usual inflection for both texts is *-ynge*, found at this time over most of England.

There are a few significant variants in the forms of the preterite: the inflection of the second person singular, especially in auxiliary verbs, is often lost in the Winchester text: this is a northern characteristic. The third person plural is usually uninflected in both texts, but Caxton shows a few examples of the southerly ending *-en*, which is not found in the MS.

Strong past participles show *-e* and *-en*, though *-e* forms (e.g. *bore* for *boren*) predominate in W. The *y-* prefix of past participles is rare in both texts, but the MS. shows more examples, usually in conjunction with the *-e* suffix (*i-sette*). This prefix and suffix normally indicates a southern or south-western origin for a text, but is also found in the central and west Midlands.

There are a few nearly constant, noticeable, but not very significant variations in the forms of irregular verbs. W, for example, uses the *o* spellings of *will* (*wolt*, *woll* for Caxton's *wylt*, *wyll*), and almost always has *ded* or *dud* for Caxton's *dyd*.

[1] The regular form in the alliterative *Morte Arthure*, its source.

Bibliographical Note

The following list is designed to supplement the Bibliographies printed in Professor Vinaver's edition of the *Works* (1947), and at the end of his chapter on Malory in *Arthurian Literature in the Middle Ages* (see below).

M. C. BRADBROOK, *Sir Thomas Malory*. (Writers and their work, No. 95, Published for the British Council and the National Book League 1958.)

D. S. BREWER, Review of *The Tale of the Death of King Arthur*, ed. E. Vinaver (Oxford, 1955) and of R. M. Lumiansky, *The Question of Unity in Malory's Morte Darthur* (Tulane University: New Orleans, 1955). *Medium Aevum* XXV (1957), pp. 22–26.

R. T. DAVIES, 'Was Pellynor unworthy?' *Notes and Queries*, N.S. iv (1957), p. 370.

J. W. GIBSON, 'The characterization of King Arthur in medieval English literature.' *v. Index to theses accepted for higher degrees*, v (1954–5), p. 137 (Sheffield).

A. GOSSMAN AND G. W. WHITING, 'King Arthur's farewell to Guinevere'. *Notes and Queries*, N.S. vi (1959), pp. 446–8.

W. L. GUERIN, 'The function of "The Death of Arthur" in Malory's tragedy of the Round Table'. *Dissertation Abstracts* xix, 2089 (Tulane).

R. M. LUMIANSKY, 'Two notes on Malory's *Morte Darthur*', *Neuphilologische Mitteilungen* lviii (1957), pp. 148–53.

—— 'Malory's use of *Le Morte Arthur* and *Mort Artu*', *Etudes Anglaises* x (1957), pp. 97–108.

—— 'Tristram's first interviews with Mark in Malory's *Morte Darthur*,' *Modern Language Notes* lxx (1955), pp. 476–8.

—— 'Malory's steadfast Bors', *Tulane Studies in English* viii (1958).

D. C. MUECKE, 'Some notes on Vinaver's Malory', *M.L.N.* lxx (1955), pp. 325–8.

R. N. RIOUX, 'Sir Thomas Malory, créateur verbal', *Etudes Anglaises* xii (1959), pp. 193–7.

T. C. RUMBLE, 'The first explicit in Malory's *Morte Darthur*', *M.L.N.* lxxi (1956), pp. 564–6.

—— 'Malory's *Works* and Vinaver's comments: some inconsistencies resolved', *Journal of English and Germanic Philology*, lix (1960), pp. 59–69.

A. O. SANDVED, 'A note on the language of Caxton's Malory and that of the Winchester MS.', *English Studies* xl (1959), pp. 113–14.

J. ŠIMKO, 'A linguistic analysis of the Winchester Manuscript and William Caxton's edition of Sir Thomas Malory's *Morte Darthur*', *Philologica* viii (1956).

—— *Word-order in the Winchester Manuscript and in William Caxton's edition of Thomas Malory's* Morte Darthur (1485): *a comparison* (Halle (Saale), 1957).

B. J. THEARLE, 'Malory in the nineteenth century', *Dissertation Abstracts* xix, 133 (Maryland).

P. E. TUCKER, 'Malory's conception of chivalry as it appears in his treatment of the story of Sir Lancelot'. *v. Index to theses accepted for higher degrees* iv (1953–4), p. 131. (Oxford).

—— 'A source for "The Healing of Sir Urry" in the *Morte Darthur*', *Modern Language Review*. l (1955), pp. 490–2.

VINAVER, E., 'Sir Thomas Malory'. *Arthurian literature in the Middle Ages: a collaborative history*, ed. R. S. Loomis (Oxford, 1959), pp. 541–52.

R. H. WILSON, 'Addenda on Malory's minor characters'. *J.E.G.P.* lv (1956), pp. 567–87.

—— 'How many books did Malory write?' *Univ. of Texas Studies in English* xxx (1951), pp. 1–23.

R. T. D.